MEAN GIRL FEMINISM

MEAN GIRL FEMINISM

How White Feminists GASLIGHT, GATEKEEP, and GIRLBOSS

KIM HONG NGUYEN

UNIVERSITY OF ILLINOIS PRESS
Urbana, Chicago, and Springfield

Publication supported by the Robert Harding and Lois
Claxton Humanities and Social Sciences Grant at the
University of Waterloo.

Library of Congress Cataloging-in-Publication Data
Names: Nguyen, Kim Hong (Kim Hong Thanh), author.
Title: Mean girl feminism : how White feminists gaslight,
    gatekeep, and girlboss / Kim Hong Nguyen.
Description: Urbana : University of Illinois Press, 2024. |
    Series: Feminist media studies | Includes bibliographical
    references and index.
Identifiers: LCCN 2023023192 (print) | LCCN
    2023023193 (ebook) | ISBN 9780252045578
    (cloth) | ISBN 9780252087684 (paperback) | ISBN
    9780252055232 (ebook)
Subjects: LCSH: White feminism—North America. |
    Feminism and racism—North America.
Classification: LCC HQ1169 .N48 2024 (print) |
    LCC HQ1169 (ebook) | DDC 305.48/809—dc23/
    eng/20230718
LC record available at https://lccn.loc.gov/2023023192
LC ebook record available at https://lccn.loc.gov/
    2023023193

Contents

Preface

Whitesplaining White Lady of Liberal Reason

In the *Saturday Night Live* (*SNL*) "Inner White Girl" (2015) sketch, Leslie Jones is given a necklace that calls on Inner White Girl (Reese Witherspoon), who spiritually guides her through white institutional ways of doing and reasoning. Jones is at a bank, upset at being charged an overdraft fee, but in the end—when she is asked to wait a few minutes after the bank realizes its mistake—Inner White Girl is the one who gets angry over the wait time. This scenario illustrates a character type I call the whitesplaining white lady of liberal reason.

Girlboss, a Self-Promotional Equity Lady

In *SNL*'s "Mean Girls" (2018), Tina Fey plays herself, excited about her movie *Mean Girls* becoming a Broadway musical. Fey tries to audition as its star, claiming to be inspired by Lin-Manuel Miranda, who wrote and then starred in the Broadway musical *Hamilton*. Fey demonstrates a character type known as the girlboss or self-promotional equity lady.

Karen with Illegible Rage

Idris Elba plays Dr. Bruce Banner, who, having been hit by gamma radiation in a failed experiment, transforms into a prototypical Karen (Cecily Strong) in *SNL*'s "Impossible Hulk" (2019). She claims to be threatened and "aggressed," and says that she "cannot breathe," echoing the words of

Eric Garner right before his death at the hands of New York police. Strong plays a prototypical Karen with illegible rage.

Power Couple Wife with Resting Bitch Face

In *SNL*'s "First Lady" (2018), Melania Trump (Cecily Strong) receives a pep talk from other first ladies. After three white ladies speak, wallowing in their subordinate status to their husbands, Michelle Obama (Leslie Jones) enters and contends that she does not share their experience of gendered mistreatment. In response to Jackie Kennedy's (Natalie Portman) suggestion to stand and clap at Donald Trump's speech, Melania says that sometimes she will sit down and not clap. Strong's Trump is an example of a white lady in a power couple with RBF (resting bitch face).

I begin with these four white women characters parodied on the sketch comedy show *Saturday Night Live* because they are examples of the white womanhood discussed in this book. Not mutually exclusive from one another, these characters illustrate the performativity of white womanhood as a kind of violence in ways that it is not marked and interpreted as such. This is what I call *mean girl feminism*. Mean girl feminism is the name of a kind of white feminism that encourages girls and women to be bitchy, sassy, sarcastic, and ironic as feminist performance.[1] But the snap, the clapback, the eye roll, and other means of being bitchy co-opt racialized performativity. From these sketch comedy examples, white womanhood is recognizable as the epitome of effective female complaint, with words that provoke fear, and harassment that arises from the instability of white feminine innocence. White womanhood is also recognizable in the ways in which white women co-opt the affect, content, and form of racialized oppression and protest, an interior knowledge denied to people of color.

I write this book to show an affective worlding of feminism that encourages white mean girls to thrive, not just survive, especially at a time when white women are "members of the richest race in the world."[2] As a kind of white feminism, mean girl feminism builds and aims to make way for strong, assertive, and aggressive women in the world, rather than seeking to foster an environment that accepts vulnerability and difference. If, as Koa Beck writes, white feminism "is anchored in the accumulation of individual power rather than the redistribution of it," then it is meanness coupled with feminism that promotes "white rage" of the modern era.[3] Being that "white rage is not about visible violence" and is triggered by Black and racialized demands for equitable opportunities at life, my motivation to write this book is not purely pedantic or academic.[4] There is no one traumatic response that has me hell-bent on writing this book.

Rather, this book is inspired by my experience with white feminist women in the academic enterprise who believe that protecting academic elitism and rigor is compatible with promoting intersectional feminist politics.[5] These white feminist women cite work-life balance and the tribulations of parenting as a rationale for being flaky, unreliable proponents of intersectional feminism. This book is inspired by my interactions with white feminist women who fashion themselves as witty, sarcastic, ironic, and too highly articulate to connect with their unfunny racialized counterparts, like Tina Fey in the *SNL* "Mean Girls" skit. This book is inspired by my encounters with white feminist women who make feminism their identity, with feminist signs in their offices, and who assume a "white woman in charge" role "when surrounded by women of color."[6] These white feminist women self-identify and brand themselves as intersectional feminist experts as a signal of their good intentions and their well-read understanding of feminist theory, rather than as a means of interracial connection and willingness to do the work of struggle and solidarity. This book is inspired by witnessing white feminists heterosexually conjoined within professorial power couples who engage in sexual violence and mobilize their professional networks to accept their questionable actions and to propagate their interests as intellectually superior, like Melania Trump in the *SNL* "First Lady" skit.[7] This book is inspired by the white women who tried to mother me when I was growing up, as if they were better than my own mother. Relatedly, this book is inspired by my white women colleagues who try to offer unsolicited mentorship or who seek out racialized colleagues as junior, not as equal, to them. This book too is inspired by my interactions with white feminist men who deem it a compliment—thanks to Joreen's *Bitch Manifesto* (1968)—to call a woman a bitch. All these white feminists gaslight, gatekeep, and girlboss in order to advance their careers, increase their social capital and networks, and overall appear as intelligent and sassy.

Anger is an important emotional reaction to injustice, and many academic intellectuals and activists have mobilized minoritized shame—about who they love and who they are—into anger for collective action and liberation. But meanness, as this book will examine, operates differently. I propose that the Karen figure is not angry, but mean. The characters and personas of Tina Fey, Taylor Swift, Reese Witherspoon, and many others may recognize the value of feminism and even wear and articulate it quite well and convincingly, but they are not angry. Meanness might be best summarized in the form of a meme that first appeared on Tumblr in early 2021, parodying white women's familiar "Live, Laugh, Love": "Gaslight (every moment), Gatekeep (every day), Girlboss (beyond words)."[8] Tumblr users and others who have adopted this phrase are not endorsing the practices of gaslighting, gatekeeping, or girlbossing. Rather, they are pointing out how white womanhood and feminism encourage these practices to help women get what they want. Girlbosses, at home or in the workplace, at the helm or in the grind, are also white women who gatekeep and protect their know-it-all brand of feminism by dictating who is feminist and the know-how of feminism. These mean girls gaslight and manipulate to achieve their goals. An example is influencer and bestselling author of *Girl, Wash Your Face* (2018) and *Girl, Stop Apologizing* (2019), Rachel Hollis. In a 2021 TikTok video, Hollis describes her girlboss drive and, in so doing, mentions she relies on a housecleaner. In response to followers' criticism that she is privileged AF and unrelatable, which she readily admits, Hollis defensively asks: "What is it about me that made you think I want to be relatable? No, sis. Literally everything I do in my life is to live a life that most people can't relate to." The posted video's caption reads: "Harriet Tubman, RBG [Ruth Bader Ginsburg], Marie Curie, Oprah Winfrey, Amelia Earhart, Frida Kahlo, Malala Yousafzai, Wu Zetian . . . all Unrelatable AF. Happy Women's History Month!"[9] A later apology notwithstanding, Hollis illustrates that what is demanded of mean girl feminism is to keep up with an image that is on par with and at the same time claims to rebel against cis-heteropatriarchy. By comparing herself to a list of white and racialized women to defend against the concern about her privilege and lack of relatability, Hollis misses the point that her grit and grind to become a girlboss depend on labor exploitation of others. Furthermore, Hollis fails to notice that someone like Harriet Tubman was aiming not for success for success's sake as feminist visibility, but for collective freedom and liberation.

Why are white women mean, so mean? Meanness borrows the virtue of anger and signals disagreement with the way the world works. Meanness articulates the feeling of anger by having the bold courage to enunciate and use language to name it. White women are exploiting the language and performativity of the minoritized at a time in which their whiteness challenges and calls into question the circumstances and extent of their oppression. In fact, toxic white womanhood deploys a victimized status as an excuse for being mean to everyone, including marginalized groups. This is not to say that white women do not experience any form of oppression; cis-hetero sexism absolutely exists and affects white women. This is to say that meanness allows white women to hold on to their victimized status without regard to context.

To write about white womanhood is to write about a confused inter-sectionality that is both marginalized as women and privileged as white. White women are encouraged to take their cues from racialized women, the work of the Combahee River Collective, and research that emerges from intersectional feminism. This intersectional encouragement can lead to new forms of appropriation and new problematic performances.[10] In addition, to write about white womanhood requires a considerate balance between the progressive value of feminism and feminism's affective expression of mean-ness. Because the difference between calling out and calling in is delicate, I turn to cultural rather than personal examples to illustrate the strategies and subsequent harms that white womanhood poses to racialized people. This is to say that toxic white womanhood is both fragile and evolving, and that racialized people are subject to problematic notions of mean girl feminism. This book utilizes a rhetorical approach in order to capture the cultural resources through which white womanhood is constructed. The texts that congeal into the feminist constructions of white womanhood are selected for their potential to demonstrate an accretion of microaggressions that have happened to me.[11] The character types from *SNL* and the characters in the texts discussed in this book are composites of my professors, my bosses, my under/graduate student peers, my coworkers, and my friends who might call themselves feminist killjoys, a moniker to be worn on weekdays and taken off as they go home to love their toxic male partners. I analyze movies, tele-vision, and other texts for how they can serve as lessons on what feminism looks like as well as what feminism refuses to name as feminist. I explore how the structure of (mis)recognition in popular feminism hinges on the performativity of womanhood and the genre of femininity.[12] As Lauren Berlant argues, femininity "brackets many kinds of structural and historical antagonism," and "gender-marked texts of women's popular culture cultivate fantasies of vague belonging as an alleviation of what is hard to manage in the lived real—social antagonisms, exploitation, compromised intimacies, the attrition of life."[13] Berlant describes how women's popular culture is built around constructing a feeling of belonging that can provide relief from the toil of everyday life (in which gender is at the root of both conflict and solution). For Berlant, femininity operates as a generic mode of engage-ment that is also a delay and a deferral to deal with lived structural and historical antagonisms. I hope that this book, which takes its examples from women's popular culture, demonstrates the everyday qualities of mean girl feminism and the way it operates as a norm and as a form of civility. What should become apparent is how, in popular culture, the "feminist" tropes of resistance traffic in a toxic white womanhood that sustains imperialist white supremacist capitalist cis-heteropatriarchy.[14]

Feminist critique is becoming a common and important feature in women's popular culture, introducing antipatriarchal values to large audiences. However, at the same time, constant critique in feminism can have the unwitting effect of producing fewer worlds.[15] Women's popular culture—and feminist theory, too—often constructs feminism as hinging on individual performativity rather than on different ways of living life in community and in relationality. As such, mean girl feminism doesn't ask what a feminist worlding should look and feel like or how feminist principles might be realized in collective daily practices. Rather, it calls into question the relationship between performativity and identity: Why is that inarticulate person *not feminist*? If she doesn't have it all and has not reached the status of a girlboss who can gaslight and gatekeep, is she feminist yet? If choice feminism is the ideology that any choice a woman makes is acceptable and should be justified—that feminism is everything—choice feminism is also a form of white feminism that makes way for mean girl feminists. There is a mean streak in feminism too that is anti-choice and anti-pleasure—that renders only certain white choices acceptable as feminist driven. Beck explains, "'feminist' conversations circle loosely around claiming feminism as one's own—rather than as an assembled body to overcome systemic barriers."[16] Sara Ahmed, too, recognizes that her own work on the feminist killjoy figure can be misconstrued as an identity *as* rather than an identity *with* whom feminism builds a world. She argues: "A killjoy becomes a manifesto when we are willing to take up this figure, to assemble a life *not as her but around her, in her company*."[17] In other words, being a killjoy is not about *you* but about *her/them*, not about being a killjoy per se but about making space for her/them, supporting her/them. It is mean girl feminism that teaches us—yes, including me—that in order to challenge power, you need to be verbally aggressive, find a counterpart to make a power couple, and so on, in ways that scaffold the popular rebirth of white feminism on the effaced figure of women of color.

In exploring how meanness is seen as antipatriarchal, this book considers the ways in which white mean girls are empowered by strict gender analysis to express their rage as a form of feminism. Mean girl feminism makes white meanness palatable by constructing patriarchal ills as aggression inducing and by recirculating that intraracial tension as an innocent pleasure. My hope is that by showing how mean girl feminism optimizes the performativity of white womanhood, this book demonstrates the contemporary problems and intersectional shortcomings of white feminism, which "can be practiced by anyone, of any race, background, allegiance, identity, and affiliation."[18] The rhetorical power of white feminism relies on meanness to do the affective work of relevant and constant critique found in women's popular culture and to dissociate white feminism from its fringes and splinter movements. I hope to show, as Beck does, that "supporters of white feminism want to reconcile their feminism with the mythology that they are still special, better, 'work harder,' and are therefore entitled to the roles that any combination of race, class privilege, conventional womanhood, and/or a cis gender have landed them."[19] Engaging with what feminism is and is not—as an assemblage of issues that make up mean girl feminism—is necessary for white feminism to move in new, productive directions, toward the intersectional ethic to which it may aspire.

Acknowledgments

This book was a long time coming, before I even knew it and started the research in earnest. I dedicate this book to my mother, Dam Thi Nguyen. In a way, one could say that it is my mom that Audre Lorde is talking about when she urges white feminists to think about the non-white women who clean their houses. A South Vietnamese refugee with few English skills, my mom was a maid to many white working bourgeois women. My mom would want me to note that they were nice people. Growing up, however, I always thought her job was weird, considering one woman would accuse her of stealing her diamond ring, then fire her . . . until she realized she misplaced it and tried to hire my mom back. She received Christmas cards thanking her for being "family" and their "best friend," written by white wealthy women much like Jean Cabot from *Crash*. When my mom announced to her employers she was retiring from the physically intensive labor, one white woman wondered whether retirement actually applied to her home because she regularly visited my mom as a "friend."

Though I have received my mom's generous permission, these are stories that she never shared with me out of anger. I learned these stories indirectly because I had to translate or read the apology/rehiring note from the woman who accused her of stealing, and the Christmas cards attached to cheap candle and toiletry gifts. Thus, for me, Lorde's acknowledgment (and so much of critical race theory) helped me understand that the economic and social challenges my family and I faced—our life chances—were directly related to the ways in which white people try to do good by employing/ befriending racialized people and projecting shared frustrations of gender on them. I also dedicate this book to my father, Hung Phuc Nguyen, who cheered me on until the very last of his days. My parents were no model minorities, but they were my model minorities.

I want to thank Gerald Voorhees, Sabrina Low, Tara DeBoer, Kishonna Gray, Frankie Condon, Katy Fulfer, Kent Ono, Vershawn Young, the two anonymous book reviewers, and also many of my University of Waterloo (UW) undergraduate students for their generous conversations and close readings of parts of this book. I have immense gratitude for the W3+: Waterloo Womxn & Nonbinary Wednesdays Coordinating Crew—Naila Ayala, Cassie Bechard, Katie Damphouse, Jordan Hale, Lowine Hill, Andrea Jonahs, Laura McDonald, Michelle Przedborski, Meghan Riley, Emily Reid-Musson, and Lauren Smith—for co-creating a space to challenge white feminism. I also appreciate the financial support from a UW/SSHRC (Social Sciences and Humanities Research Council) travel grant, HeForShe travel grant, the Faculty of Arts Dean's Office, led by Doug Peers, and the Robert Harding & Lois Claxton Humanities and Social Sciences Grant. My presentations to the UW Gender and Social Justice program and the Women's Centre helped me shape and develop my analysis of mean girl feminism. I also want to thank University of Illinois Press editors Daniel Nasset and Mariah Mendes Schaefer and Feminist Media Studies series editor Rebecca Wanzo and the Feminist Media Studies series editorial board for their confidence in this project. Special thanks goes to my writing coach, Nadine Fladd, who tirelessly guided me from the book's conception to its end, read multiple drafts of my chapters, and pushed the ideas expressed here into clarity. Finally, but definitely not least, I thank all of my family for their unwavering love.

MEAN GIRL FEMINISM

FEMINIST CIVILITY AND THE RIGHT TO BE MEAN

The camera pans wide to reveal red curtains spreading open over a stage. Country musician Taylor Swift appears, accusing in her white feminine voice: "You! with your words like knives / And swords and weapons that you use against me / You have knocked me off my feet again / Got me feeling like a-nothing." Her band plays banjos and tambourines in a backcountry setting of the American South in the opening scene. The music video of "Mean" (2011) depicts a white queer boy bullied by the football team, a white waitress working to save for a university degree, a white short-haired girl excluded from lunch conversation because of her blue ribbon (symbolic of counter-hegemonic womanhood), and Swift herself, tied to railroad tracks in front of her white drunk boyfriend. The chorus jubilantly twangs in high relief, "Someday I'll be living in a big old city / And all you're ever gonna be is mean." This is when Swift interrupts the tempo of the song to avenge mean-ness with the master's tools: "All you are is mean / And a liar / And pathetic / And alone in life / And mean, and mean, and mean, and mean." The setting changes to depict neoliberal notions of success, with Swift's band playing on Broadway in New York City, the bullied boy now fashion designer, the server now corporate executive, and Swift removing the ropes, which were never secured in the first place.[1] "Mean" ends with the young girl with the blue ribbon applauding Swift's performance onstage. Like her other songs, "Mean" is illustrative of the celebrity persona that Swift has been known for and called out on: someone who uses songwriting as an entrepreneurial outlet for getting crossed, and markets herself as a white woman victimized by her now-former boyfriends (and, more recently, as an "antihero" who ironically can recognize that she is the problem).[2] At the same time, it is she who loves him; it is white colonial womanhood that loves and tempers white masculinity. Labeling bullying and verbal assaults as "mean," Swift suggests that meanness governs gendered and sexual inclusion into a heteronormative, racialized, and classed subjectivity.

This song, situated in relation to Swift's celebrity, shows us a microcosm of the productive power of mean girl feminism: that is, how white women inhabit a moral domain of virtue that enables feminism to function as embourgeoisement, a neoliberal form of racial and gendered advancement.[3] Mean girl feminism offers a noble revival of white heteronormative womanhood amid white rage by allowing white women to "reclaim" bitchiness as feminist performativity, thereby distancing white women from the discourse of racist microaggressions. White colonial privilege in the song motivates the neoliberal movement from a small country town to the big city, from minimum wage to salary, and from relationally bounded to individual and free. Swift's solution of calling out (his) individual meanness imbues colonial structures of sovereignty with feminist appeal and positive affect, as if imperialist white capitalist cis-heteropatriarchy is not mean and can be hospitable to the marginalized. Once a recipient of meanness, Swift, empowered through song and the commercial white male gaze, demonstrates how presenting oneself as innocent when dealing with sexism is the condition of possibility for her own meanness.

Taylor Swift is a useful starting point to illustrate the performative contradiction of naming mean girl feminism into existence, including in my own effort to discuss her. I recognize that to accuse the mean girl of meanness is a kind of meanness itself. However, it is this open secret about Swift that makes her an exemplar of mean girl feminism. Her damsel-in-distress persona is, on the one hand, a familiar trope, and, on the other hand, a ploy to hide her own white meanness. Kanye West's disruption of her award acceptance speech in 2009 is infamous. But so, too, is what happened years later, after West referenced Swift in his song "Famous" (2016). Swift publicly denied approving the lyric, until West's then wife Kim Kardashian released a recording of a phone call to the contrary. To many, this incident is an illustration of white duplicity. White duplicity is all too familiar for racialized folks. The damsel in distress always has been a mean girl in white supremacy, a duality that whiteness has denied but that now feminism hails.

The music and celebrity of Taylor Swift exemplify the very kind of problem that gender studies and white liberal feminism create and purport to solve. This book considers how meanness and other negative feelings normalize white women's performativity and communication practices as feminist and antipatriarchal. My purpose is to explore how feminism points to gender as if it is resistance in and of itself. Examining feminist discourses of mean girls and women that leverage heteronormative gender performativity, I argue that feminism positions the white mean girl as the idealistic figure of complaint and of mature civility. Feminism imagines scenarios that require the category of gender for understanding cis-heteropatriarchy and proposes that cis-heteropatriarchy should be confronted and countered with meanness. At the crux, feminism identifies the mean girl as cis-heteropatriarchy's enemy and at the same time argues that the mean girl is the very figure whose performativity is patriarchy's needed fix. Feminism contends that mean girls are cis-heteropatriarchy's problem because they violate the norms and dictates of womanhood. At the same time, ironically and cheekily, feminism poses mean civility as a form of agency that displaces and resists cis-heteropatriarchy. In mean girl feminism, the mean girl comes to represent a new kind of sovereignty—a better master and a more equitable interest in power—by donning non-white racialization and wearing features of Blackness in order to dramatize confrontations with cis-heteropatriarchy.

As Koa Beck explains, "for white feminism (as well as white and white-passing women), protest is a safe endeavor."[4] Mean girl feminism encourages the performativity of white womanhood as aggression.[5] While I track meanness as specific to mean girl feminism, this is an era in which neoliberal capitalism and other forms of disciplinary power have naturalized interpersonal discursive violence. *Toronto Star*'s Vinay Menon wonders whether we live in a "culture of meanness," where nastiness and fighting might be contagious.[6] Scholar Melissa Gregg argues that neoliberal working conditions encourage workers to depersonalize and reduce human interaction, favoring "user friendly" communication that is technically, not genuinely, friendly.[7] Email and other textual-based messaging stand in for interpersonal contact and relationality, leaving little room for coalition building and discourse about work conditions, and expanding the possibility for meanness. Soraya Roberts of *Yahoo News* speculates that meanness is the common attribute for the highest-earning media personalities topping the Forbes list.[8] The culture of meanness and discursive violence bolsters neoliberal values of individualism and a laissez-faire approach to systemic inequities of imperialist white supremacist capitalist cis-heteropatriarchy. Scholars of mediated violence have discussed how violent video games that target terrorists or criminals grew in popularity over those that target aliens and fantastical creatures.[9] The shift to depicting violence against humans and stereotypical images reproduces the decentralization of colonial violence that has marked the modern era. Where Michel Foucault considers liberalism to be a nascent form of racism emerging with the decline of monarchies and absolutism, Ann Laura Stoler and other scholars point to this nineteenth-century period of monarchical decline and liberalism's rise as colonial racism's modern form. Stoler calls the replacement of violent autocracy with so-called nonviolent governmental practices "embourgeoisement" to describe how white settler women and white nuclear family expectations became interpellated into colonial governance.[10] Stoler's research on decentralized colonial violence shows how imperial concerns about gender are infused with and empowered by colonialism's investment in racialized hierarchies, eugenic science, etiquette rules, and social expectations. Whereas Gabrielle Moss and other feminist scholars note that girls are seen as the source of blame for a culture of meanness and stereotyped as meaner and more aggressive than boys, Stoler suggests that meanness performed by white girls and women fosters the perception of nonviolence characteristic of colonial societies.[11]

What women can do, say, or wear, and where women can go, work, or play: all these have been topics that white liberal feminism has tried to bend, expand, and render boundless to create a damsel in resistance, in response to stereotypes of white women as nice, patient homemakers to petulant children and ungrateful husbands. Perhaps performativity was a way of answering Hélène Cixous's feminist call to "write about women and bring women to writing," which would allow a woman to "return to the body which has been more than confiscated from her, which has been turned into the uncanny stranger on display."[12] However, on display are not just gendered bodies, but white bodies, as white women are positioned to fulfill and circulate the promise of feminism. When Justin Trudeau took office as prime minister in 2015, he formed the first male/female gender-balanced cabinet in Canadian history. Framed as a gender issue, work-life balance is resolved by including white entrepreneurial women ready to assert their needs, like Sheryl Sandberg in *Lean In: Women, Work, and the Will to Lead*, even though women of color have always been leaning in.[13] In 2014, turning protest into fashion, mostly white models carried signs on Chanel's runway emblazoned with "Feminism Not Masochism," "Ladies First," and "History Is Her Story." In university classrooms, making up the general sense of diversity and the primary beneficiaries of affirmative action policy are white women.[14] Unfortunately, the gender-only feminism that allows for the inclusion of white women in education, in the workplace, in politics, and in the media is interpreted not as a continuation of white prestige and a product of white women's embourgeoisement, but as a positive effect of liberal feminism on patriarchal power.[15] As Beck explains:

> This approach makes it okay, even celebratory, to hinge all your energies and hopes for social justice on a young female CEO who doesn't push for

decent healthcare benefits. It makes it sufficient that she only acts with her own job performance and product metrics, and exploits the underpaid, overextended work of everyone else in the company to get there. It makes it fine that she relies on a steady stream of immigrant nannies so that she can do this work. Because change will come one woman at a time. We support feminism by supporting the singularity of her.[16]

Although the groundbreaking and much-cited works of queer scholars Judith Butler and José Muñoz hinge on challenging gender essentialism, the feminist struggle of being a woman in a man's world and demanding inclusion in public institutions (efforts undertaken to widen women's capacity for agency) has prompted theories and criticism about traditional gender performativity and other means of communicating womanhood. Many discourses of feminist performativity ignore their important insights on gender performativity as queer and trans interventions in order to resecure a feminism that makes way for (re)iterating heteronormativity, whiteness, and "visible, epidermal iconography of difference to the commodity tableau of contemporary technologies . . . [in ways that] undermine political analyses that pivot on the exclusion, silence, or invisibility of various groups and their histories."[17]

Feminism is incapable of solving the major problem to which its existence gives rise: the problem of heterosexism and of the gender binary and differentiation. Reducing the production of identity into a sex binary, feminism allows race to be erased and rendered irrelevant. Ruby Hamad explains that white womanhood helps maintain white dominance by refusing to dismantle the binary of sex differentiation that disempowers all, including white women themselves.[18] Feminist values have led to woman-centered and woman-produced dramas, gender studies programs, research on gender disparity, and political organizations and activism to end discrimination. But this feminism's woman-centeredness, combined with sex differentiation, has gone awry in North America. Indeed, a different tenor of gender inequity seeks our attention. Efforts to recognize women's potential as capable leaders and creative visionaries can be bought cheaply with T-shirts and mugs emblazoned with slogans like "Act like a Lady, Think like a Boss." Just as popular is the neologism *boss bitch* and a burgeoning self-help section for women to strategize in their career and other realms and to embrace the sassy, mean girl within them. Blockbuster woman-authored movies like *Mean Girls* (2004) and controversial but widely popular television series like *Gossip Girl* (2007–12) dramatize mean white girls vying for the top of the social hierarchy. When Sarah Palin was selected as the Republican nominee for vice president in 2008, she was called a mean girl and simultaneously accused the media of being mean spirited, prompting liberal Melissa McEwan's launch of the blog post series Sarah Palin Sexism Watch.[19] Likewise, gender studies has examined the mean girl as both a sign of postfeminism and the figure limiting feminist advancement. By centering women, feminism allows white women to reconcile their own heterosexuality and cisgender as a form of rebellion and protects mean women who gatekeep and exclude queer and trans peoples and issues. Sara Ahmed, too, recognizes feminism gone awry— or what I am calling mean girl feminism—when she not only emphatically calls on feminists to follow Audre Lorde's call to arms ("do not become the master's tool!") but also discusses feminism's use of "the 'willfulness charge' to create an impression, that of being lonely radical feminist voices struggling against the tide of social opinion. They have used this impression of having to struggle against to articulate a position against trans people, who have to struggle to exist, a position articulated so vehemently that it could only be described as hate speech."[20]

In addition, feminism ignores the very condition that makes feminism necessary in the first place: the production of the subaltern and those who cannot articulate their interior knowledge in intelligible ways. As Alexander Weheliye states, "What is at stake is not so much the lack of language per se, since we have known for a while now that the subaltern cannot speak, but the kinds of dialects available to the subjected and how these are seen and heard by those who bear witness to their plight."[21] Indeed, feminist celebration of the articulate tongue as "the organ of feminist rebellion" is ableist.[22] Jay Dolmage discusses how the process of confronting academic elitism involves requiring marginalized students to articulate their needs, identify their problems, and offer solutions.[23] Ahmed advises that we "*learn how to hear what is impossible*. Such an impossible hearing is only possible if we respond to a pain that we cannot claim as our own."[24]

Following Jessie Daniels's argument that white feminism is not a monolith but has many variants, I want to look at a particular kind of white feminism that has gone awry.[25] Using mean girl discourses as the focus of study, I ask: What functions does meanness generate for feminism? In what ways does meanness enable feminism to have a resistant tenor? What is being foreclosed in order for one to become a feminist subject? I ask these questions because I want to consider how resistance is harder to locate and how feminist liberation is more difficult to imagine in the era of mean girl feminism. Taking as a point of departure Stoler's concept of embourgeoisement as a form of decentralized violence, I ask how feminism is part of the white colonial project to create workers committed to capitalism, loving subjects in cis-heteropatriarchy, and white feminine women whose toxicity is protected by the category of sex-binary gender. I want to explore how gender inequity—the ways white feminism pushes to recognize it, the assumed sources of it, the solutions that remedy it—perpetuates and produces racial harm. If, as Hamad has argued, the damsel in distress takes the innocence of people of color for herself by rendering people of color as targets of violence, then the figure of the mean girl takes the tropology of resistance for herself by stealing racialized modes of protest.[26] Like Taylor Swift in her music video "Mean," mean girl feminism frees the damsel in distress bound by cis-heteropatriarchy by transforming her into a damsel in resistance who performs tactics of racialized resistance to gendered oppression.

Expanding gender performativity to include the right to be mean is the new frontier for white feminist discontent, but in that frontier there lies feminism's main fault line of nonperformativity. Following Ahmed's model of the nonperformative, I suggest that white women's performativity "works precisely by not bringing about the effects that they name."[27] I approach this feminist turn to performativity beginning in the 1970s as a heteronormative flirt with cis-heteropatriarchy itself.[28] Gender performativity in feminism is a nonperformativity that aims to bring about a world that emphasizes individual performance, wits, and smarts, above community resilience and solidarity.

By analyzing post-1970 and post–civil rights discourses that figure mean girls/women as patriarchy's antagonists and solutions, I show that feminism is not merely a site that produces the gendered self, which is always already an impossible notion that cannot occur in isolation from other axes of identity or its historical milieu. Rather, feminism is a site that produces the genre of gender for a white subjectivity by figuring meanness as antipatriarchal performativity. I argue that meanness disciplines feminism into networks of white affection. In its focus on performativity instead of anticolonial freedom and decolonial liberation, mean girl feminism mobilizes narcissism as a component of its identity politics. Posed as cis-heteropatriarchy's enemy and its fix, the mean girl figure evokes a narrative of feminist progress as rebellion, at the same time her main character energy presents as a girlboss who gaslights and gatekeeps absolves white people from attending to their own violence in upholding current systems of oppression.

Over the course of this book, I illustrate how feminism develops its own notion of oppression based on gender by discounting racialization and disavowing knowledge about racialized oppression in order to position white women as the best sovereigns or equal masters of power to white men. Daniels puts it bluntly: "Some of the most ardent proponents of the idea that talking about race is divisive that I've encountered are white feminists."[29]

White feminists who do not think they are the problem are the hardest to convince they, indeed, are the problem. I extend the work of Stoler, Angela Davis, Sabine Broeck, Alexander Weheliye, and many others who complicate the field of gender studies, the role white women play in the making of Western institutions, and, in a word, feminism. Enslavism (and white women's co-optation of Black enslavement to mark their own oppression), the failure to credit ideas to Black women, white global motherhood, and white neoliberal heterorelationality vis-à-vis power coupledom are among the rhetorical strategies deployed to advance white women and circulate the promise of feminism. Mean girl feminism encourages white women to refuse to see their own problematic selves, refuse to admit they are the problem, or, even if or after they have admitted it, like Taylor Swift herself, refuse to do anything about it.

I select post-1970s and post–civil rights era discourses that turn to performativity and the right to be mean for their feminist potential. The feminist turn to performativity marks an anxiety about what feminism is, who can be part of feminism, what feminist practice looks like, and to what ends it works. As a nonperformative, meanness both signals an authentic commitment to feminism and at the same time obscures the harms created by a strict dedication to gender equity. What I intend on problematizing is how mean girl feminism does not create or operationalize a feminism aimed at undoing oppression. Mean girl feminism gaslights, gatekeeps, and girlbosses by putting her girl squad, her articulateness, her power couple partner, and her mothering of those she deems worthy—all for her success and advancement. The performative turn in feminism and gender studies is itself a performative politics and a nonperformative, as it too refuses to articulate a cultural and sociopolitical vision of feminism for collective freedom and liberation.

The Civility of White Liberal Feminism

As the vulnerability of oppressed white women in male-dominated spaces becomes part of the social consciousness, the impact of that vulnerability needs to be understood and tracked—and certain white scholars have indeed raised concern about toxic white womanhood (Laura Kipnis, Wendy Brown, Louise Michele Newman, Kyla Schuller, and Jack Halberstam, among others).[30] As Mamta Motwani Accapadi explains of this nuanced helplessness, "White women can be both helpless without the helplessness being a reflection of all White people and powerful by occupying a position of power as any White person."[31] What Stoler wrote in her case study of late nineteenth- and early twentieth-century European colonies in South Asia is as relevant now in twenty-first-century North America: "European women are not only the true bearers of racist beliefs but also hard-line operatives who put racism into practice, encouraging class distinctions among whites while fostering new racial antagonisms, formerly muted by sexual access."[32] As the prototype of womanhood, white women have secured their economic and social station by demanding institutional supports, reformed laws, and preemptive or punitive correctives quite harmful to people of color. And yet their role here tends to be overlooked: Stephanie Jones-Rogers, for example, traces how historians ignore the role that white women played in slavery, based on the assumption that sexism legally, economically, and socially prevented women from slaveholding. Jones-Rogers documents how the commitment to white supremacy's fungibility of Black people was buttressed by white women as much as, if not more than, white men.[33] Wendy Anderson, similarly, explains the important role of white women in perpetuating white supremacist structures: "White women can be framed as the victim, the object of desire, the vessel as a means to advocate for their support of white supremacy."[34] Thus, by the start of the twentieth century, "white women were situated at the center of a new kind of 'moral order,' posed as the foundation of white propagation."[35] In her study on how white women came together as mothers and wives to "protect" their families and their nation-state from the racialized other in segregation efforts in the American South, Elizabeth Gillespie McRae puts it succinctly: "On the ground, it was often white women who shaped and sustained white supremacist politics."[36] Ruby Hamad shows that the relationship between white womanhood, feminism, and white supremacy is advantageous for white women's advancement: "White women can oscillate between their gender and their race, between being the oppressed and the oppressor."[37] Schuller argues that "the trouble with white feminism is not what it fails to address and whom it leaves out . . . [but] what it does and whom it suppresses."[38] These scholars suggest that civility is central to the racialized work of white women and their gatekeeping of class distinction, social interaction, and civic engagement.

In her argument about the feminist agenda to eliminate female inadequacy, Kipnis explains, "Femininity was the method for creatively transforming female disadvantages into advantages, basically by doing what it took to form strategic alliances with men."[39] This agenda was inherently opposed to Black feminism, as Koa Beck writes: "Behaving like men or obtaining what men have or achieving parity with men was (and still is) not only shortsighted, it was deemed innately oppressive and therefore not in line with Black feminism. After all, the machinations that make what men have and how they historically operate—patriarchy—possible relies on the exploitation of others."[40] Underwriting feminist mainstreaming is a whitewashed fairy tale that claims feminism's moral aim was and is to create equality among men and women. According to this colonial fiction, cis-heteropatriarchy created two primary injustices: political disenfranchisement through voter exclusion, and workplace discrimination through pay inequities and role disparities. White suffragettes in the United States, led by activists such as Susan B. Anthony, felt justified in their racism, buoyed by the righteous goal of gender equality. Newman documents how suffrage mobilization was rooted in white worries about racial advancement of Black, Indigenous, and Asian populations.[41] Beck eloquently argues that the first wave's "insistence on sexism only would be an essential and enduring divide between white feminists and literally everyone else: queer, non-white, and working-class feminisms. It's a defining characteristic of white feminist mobilization in every successive wave, and foundational to how they would continue to both fight for and envision gender equality."[42] Instead of industrializing domestic labor, as Davis advocates, feminism urges white women to enter the workplace and to use and employ immigrant women and women of color to clean their homes, while saving their marriages and heteronormative image of blissful coexistence.[43] And the repercussions are global: amid the Persian Gulf War (1990–91), for example, the National Organization for Women and Planned Parenthood kept antiwar criticism to a minimum by focusing on the problems of cis-heteropatriarchy there and by presenting women of color as silent benefactors of feminism.[44] Feminism is part of a long-standing colonial history where white women act as gatekeepers of sexuality, gender, race, and class in order to secure their own status and credibility.

In a chapter entitled "White Women's Tears," Robin DiAngelo considers that "when forced to do so, white men could acknowledge white women's humanity; white women were their sisters, wives, and daughters. And of course, through these relationships, white women's increased access to resources benefited white men."[45] This increased access to resources takes us back to Stoler's notion of embourgeoisement, which she uses to theorize white women's roles in colony development and how (as Vron Ware writes) "gender played a crucial role in organizing ideas of 'race' and 'civilization', and women were involved in the expansion and maintenance of the Empire."[46] Embourgeoisement is the colonial process in which white women sought European prestige and status alongside white men.[47] Although its original meaning is simply the empirical convergence of the working class and middle class through the former's adoption of middle-class values, beliefs, and consumption styles, embourgeoisement for Stoler marks the entrenched stratification in European colonies of Southeast Asia through a coalescence of white feminine vulnerability, white prestige, and racial tensions. Aspiring for better lives and enjoying newfound privileges, settler women arriving to the colonies insisted on private quarters, metropolitan amenities, and racial etiquette to gatekeep sexualized anxieties toward Natives. Embourgeoisement helped inaugurate a colonial civility that seemed nonviolent and progressive, creating racial boundaries that would produce a bourgeois settler subjectivity and stabilize colonial governance.[48] The "progressive reforms" of embourgeoisement altered the various practices of violent colonial oppression by organizing power relations among and between Indigenous peoples and settlers.[49] In the contemporary metropole, embourgeoisement endures in cultural prejudices, urban gentrification, and suburban fence lines that imply that "nice" and "clean" aesthetics are a result of white moral bourgeois people—especially women—living comfortably there, and of non-white and working-class people living elsewhere.[50]

Cecily Jones affirms that striving for recognition entails a nuanced approach to the relationship between gender and race: "Representations of white colonial women as victims of patriarchy can illuminate white male power over white feminine identities, bodies and sexualities, but do little to further understanding of the ways in which gender is mediated by race, nor the ways in which those who are constructed as social objects may seek to challenge their defined status in their quests for subjecthood."[51] Following Schuller's argument that the white feminist movement is "powered by the fantasy that white women's participation would improve civilization itself," I ask how feminism operates as a progressive reform of embourgeoisement that enhances the moral character of modern governmentality.[52] That is: How does feminism alter colonial oppression by reorganizing power relations and perceptions of white women's civilizing roles? In what ways do feminist performativity and other communication practices aimed at expanding the politics of recognition to include mean girls and women contribute to embourgeoisement? While I cannot provide a complete sketch of how feminism functions as a technology of colonial governmentality, I chart how post-1970s discourses on feminist performatives contribute to civility and to the process of modern embourgeoisement.

Civility functions as a social mediator that elicits feelings of fairness and equity by dispersing power through performativity. Old forms of civility, like traditional etiquette and manners, are less operative in modern democratic societies, which value egalitarianism and individual will and therefore make it more difficult to discern power relations. As opening doors and other historical acts of servitude become less structured along class, gender, and racial lines, the presence of chivalrous gestures or correct meal etiquette is no longer a useful indication of power's proximity and distance. Instead, modern civility involves slurs, curt retorts, strategic disavowals, and negative feelings to manage social relations. Anger is a healthy response to discrimination, unhappiness to social and institutional rejection, envy to inequality.[53] Meanness conveys and responds to the feeling of being close to or far from power. Calling women of color mean or referring to them as bitches is an effort to put them in their place, to remind them of their distance to power, to position oneself as a power-holder, and to disperse power through social relationships.

Thus, I take issue with the way that common parlance views civility as an alternative to friction, for all social relationships in colonial sovereignty are subject to civility. I thus disagree with Giorgio Agamben when he uses civility in this colloquial way, explaining that in the state of exception (or extension of state power, like a colony), the agents of the state are the arbiters of equitable application of the law, and the question of whether atrocities happen largely depends on "civility and ethical sense of the police who temporarily act as sovereign." He writes, "For life under a law that is in force without signifying resembles life in the state of exception, in which the most innocent gesture or the smallest forgetfulness can have most extreme consequences."[54] In contrast with Agamben, who views civility as something that is at odds with brute force, rendered precarious in the state of exception, Benet Davetian turns further backward in time to show how civility (along with the practices of courtesy) was conceived in early medieval Europe as a "process of deference and adulation intended to legitimize the rights claimed by the new chieftains." According to historical documents on medieval courtesy, power shifted at this time, away from male brute force and toward the aristocratic distinction of the sovereign.[55] Chivalry not only tempered male violence by redirecting it in accordance with the sovereign's wishes, but also mediated gender relations within the sovereign's court. From etiquette to manners, from the art of conversation in salons and cafés to politeness, the various codes and categories of civility are tools for preserving status and for establishing hierarchy between nobility and the nonaristocratic classes. Thus, civility and the mechanisms that regulate courteous behavior were developed not just because the sovereign needed to control and direct violence into advantageous outlets, but also because the sovereign represented nonmilitary individuals, groups, and institutions. Davetian concludes, "We are better off viewing civility as a bilateral process involving restraint on one hand and aggression and tactical behaviour on the other."[56] In other words, civility is not, as Agamben suggests, a precarious process that is absent in cultures that experience conflict, societies with divisive politics, or fascist and totalitarian governments. Civility is central to how all regimes of power govern through violence.

Tavia Nyong'o and Kyla Wazana Tompkins argue, "civility is the affective shape of administrative violence."[57] Civility constitutes the space of interpersonal relations, keeping subjects in line, justifying the exclusion of some and not others, and discouraging specific behavior. Key to civility's appeal is that it both affirms the spectacle of sovereign power and defers judgment to the force of law. That is, civility displays sovereign power's dispersion on subjects, and conjures up institutional forms of power as ideal neutral instruments of bearing judgment on and about its subjects. Thus, the demand for more "civility" arises when meanness is doing civility's work of parsing status and appropriate performativity: *let's be civil in our disagreement.* At the same time, the demand for more "civility" also arises when meanness points to (and threatens) the precarity of power relations: *she is being uncivil and out of line.* In short, a demand for more "civility" is more often than not a call for communication that is disciplined toward normal lines of intelligibility and power, not a call for niceness or nonviolence.

Rules of behavior such as saying please and avoiding politics in conversation normalize proximity and distance to sovereignty while magnifying identity and embodiment of those deserving of power's mercy. Schuller explains what I am calling feminist civility:

> Under white feminism, the goal of gender justice shrinks to defending women's qualities and identities. The agenda today becomes empowering individual women to own their voice, refuse to be mansplained to, and embrace their right to equality with men. These are fine practices on their own, but they do not convey the devastating nature of sexism, nor do they offer realistic methods of demolishing it. In fact, fetishizing the identity of Woman as the basis of feminist politics actually makes it more difficult to recognize sexism as a structure of exploitation and extraction.[58]

Rather than remembering the source and the history of pain, white feminism fetishizes womanhood by transforming the wound into an identity. Ahmed, following Wendy Brown, counsels that the problem with overinvesting in the wound makes revenge a reaction, which also makes action impossible.[59] Feminist civility maintains social relations by encouraging white women to negotiate the affective environment about the regime's decisions not with action but with meanness. If decorum and the art of conversation reveal privilege and cultural training, then meanness shows the possibilities and limits of a sovereign's graces. When white women enact meanness, they remind others of their relation to sovereign power, showing that they are capable of violence, and that they too should be feared. Daniels states, "One gesture of my white lady finger at someone darker, a request to speak to the manager, a call to 911, and my body becomes an assault weapon."[60] As a type of civility, feminist meanness impresses on the subjects of sovereign power this power's potential to turn physically violent, and it encourages docile comportment to norms. If manners, courtesy, and codes of conduct provide the oil for the smooth operation of power's machinery, then meanness is the inertia that obliges the regime to recalibrate its force, its sound, its image to support the embourgeoisement of white women. If, as Lauren Berlant notes, affective attachments have an optimistic texture that has subjects coming back to them, holding on, and remaking them even in the face of disappointment, then meanness helps subjects negotiate the failure of those very attachments.[61] Civility and its modern feminist forms of meanness—Bitch performativity, mean girl feminism, power coupledom, global motherhood—are modalities of resistance that structure optimism, and gender equality is the receding horizon that keeps subjects holding on.

Feminism has become the show—the stage—of power's fulfillment of equity. Feminist civility is best encapsulated in Swift's "Mean" video and her other work, where meanness is an outlet for gender inequity that obscures how feminism advances class mobility and white settler privilege. In the performative contradiction that is mean girl feminism (being mean and calling out meanness), Swift becomes the ideal complainer, who can perform toxic white womanhood that is both vulnerable and innocent due to sexism and mean and resistant due to feminism. Similarly, as a professor, I have found that gender studies and its courses are ideal venues for white women because feminism allows them to both affirm their own white fragility and fetishize womanhood. Feminism appears to be nonviolently and progressively addressing cis-heteropatriarchy through a performative turn that has women only leaning in more and working harder at identifying with the correct signifiers of feminism. Feminist meanness displaces attention to colonial violence and proximity to the sovereign with attention to the categories of gender and feminism themselves.

The Whiteness of Feminist Civility

Mean girl feminism regulates the relationship between white women and white men as antagonistic and unequal rather than as synchronized and cooperative. As a contemporary type of civility, feminist meanness organizes the intersection between contemporary power relations and the grid of intelligibility, and between identity, the preservation of status, and white supremacy. Alongside coworkers committing microaggressions in the workplace, friends who shade, and ghosts who never respond on the dating scene are figures of a different sort, proffering acts of positive reinforcement and civility: royals who break rules around touch by shaking hands with their subjects, presidents who high-five children and hug infants visiting the White House, celebrities who offer tours of their homes to television audiences. Continued or renewed appreciation for heads of state who overshare and engage directly with the public, and admiration for celebrities who have the time, energy, and general privilege to speak patiently with their fans, is the norm when the negative civility and reinforcement of the law is delegated and dispersed to everyone else, from police officers and border guards to trolls in politics and cyberbullies on the web.[62]

No less important to the dispersal of disciplinary power is feminism's commitment to equity for white women, which sets embourgeoisement in motion. White feminism obscures how embourgeoisement reproduces toxic white womanhood by both rendering white women vulnerable within cis-heteropatriarchy and empowering white women to enact meanness. Feminist meanness contributes to the very hardening of racialization and racial assemblage that, according to Alexander Weheliye, "discipline humanity into full humans, not-quite-humans, and nonhumans."[63] Indeed, toxic white womanhood has had persistent though largely unexamined rhetorical power, with historically violent effects on people of color. The stereotype of violent non-white intruders and rapists has been prevalent in media for decades, from movies like *The Birth of a Nation* (1915) to crime dramas like *CSI: Crime Scene Investigation* (2000–2015).[64] This enduring fiction creates a culture that accepts the cruel murder of Emmett Till (a Black boy accused of whistling at a white woman in 1955) and the premature death of Colten Boushie (an Indigenous man accused of trespassing on white property in 2016). The safety of white women underpins the punitive logics that sustain this violence against Black and Indigenous people and other people of color. In Robin DiAngelo's succinct words, "Our [white] tears trigger the terrorism of this history, particularly for African Americans."[65] In addition to voting en masse for Donald Trump in 2016 and 2020, white women have called the police on people of color for doing normal things like barbecuing and, skewing perceptions around rape, have lied to accuse men of color of rape.[66] Recently, this toxic white womanhood has been memed as "Karen" by Black Twitter to name how white women deploy their vulnerability as a tool to harm people of color. Her tantrums and meltdowns encourage people to cower and cringe, carefully walking on the eggshells of her white fragility. I am cautious in invoking the Karen meme: it can tend to scapegoat and condemn some white women as fringe and extreme, deflecting from the ubiquity of toxic white womanhood. Nevertheless, the Karen meme points to how white women can be the biggest protesters, radicals, and enforcers of the law because they know and are willing to use their body as a weapon. To put it plainly, white women are damsels to other white people, but mean girls to non-white people. Where the tearful damsel in distress provokes patriarchal protection and silences criticism of her character, the feminist damsel in resistance is the mean girl who threatens with fear and disgust. The Karen meme, Taylor Swift, characters in *Gossip Girl*, and many more white women, their representations, and their feminist programs participate in gatekeeping, gaslighting, and girlbossing through the performativity of meanness.

In its aim to extend the rights and privileges of men to women, feminism leaves undisputed the model of the idealized positive subject: the white, heterosexual, bourgeois male of enlightened reason. Scholars guided by Sylvia Wynter's work have argued that the concept of gender that founds and activates feminism is anti-Black. Where the genre of Man was challenged to the core as a gendered way of thinking and being (mankind versus humankind, for example), Wynter argues that so too should the genre of feminism be challenged as a racialized way of thinking and being.[67] Feminism is a mere reversal of an already problematic binary: that is, if the genre of Man is principled as rational, enlightened, and universal, then the genre of Woman is moralized as the frustrated (and frustrating) condition to the critique of Man. As Wynter worries about Man "overrepresent[ing] itself as if it were the human itself, and that of securing the well-being, and therefore the full cognitive and behavioral autonomy of the human species itself/ourselves," I also worry about Woman as overrepresenting itself as if it were emancipation itself, free of sovereignty.[68] In overrepresenting itself, Woman has become the master signifier of liberation, and, as Rafia Zakaria explains, "the conduit through which emancipation must flow."[69] Indeed, we should worry about Woman being used to signify both vulnerable positionality and at the same time the promise of colonialism's humanity and benevolence.

Along with the persistent refusal to cite and productively engage with Black and racialized theoretical interventions, gender studies in the West, according to Sabine Broeck, is animated by enslavism, where the Black enslaved subject "provide[s] the metaphorical horizon of what woman, if she was to achieve fully human status, was not to be."[70] Feminist theory and fiction participate in enslavism when they imagine white women as enslaved in order to create feminism. Gender studies in the West deploys the conditions, consciousness, and aspects of captivity—and all the various ways in which the Black enslaved subject has come to signify—as its negative point of reference and analogical counterpoint. By arguing that white women were not slaves, feminism could position the category of woman as compatible with and capable of the enlightened reasoning that was exclusively attributed to white male landowners. Broeck explains how enslavism was essential to the conceptualizing of gender: "A progressive and liberatory textual concept of women's genderedness—a concept to write woman into Enlightenment as a subject, that is a mode to create intelligibility for the female complaint and her demand—emerges by way of writing woman as *not* a slave."[71] Thus, the concept of gender developed in order to support the embourgeoisement of white women—to argue for the extension of rights, to redirect domestic labor to racialized women, and to ensure that white women's talent and energy were maximized in ways that were anything but all that was associated with enslaved subjects. Broeck's insights about gender studies' metaphorizing of slavery reiterate Angela Davis's observations of how, historically, white women with "unfulfilling domestic lives" have marshaled support for women's rights: "It was the women of means who invoked the analogy of slavery most literally in their effort to express the oppressive nature of marriage. . . . The early feminists may well have described marriage as 'slavery' of the same sort Black people suffered primarily for the shock value of the comparison—fearing that the seriousness of their protest might otherwise be missed."[72] Karen Sánchez-Eppler agrees that the rhetorical pairing of woman and slave, marriage and slavery, in early nineteenth-century writings and speeches from Angelina Grimké, Elizabeth Cady Stanton, Susan B. Anthony, and others "tend toward asymmetry and exploitation" by "obliterat[ing] the particularity of black and female experience" and by emphasizing sexual victimization to "project the white woman's sexual anxieties onto the sexualized body of the female slave."[73] The use of slavery as a metaphor for gender oppression illustrates how the oppression of Black people is not only disavowed by but also made central to the reproduction and legitimation of white feminist embourgeoisement. In this way, feminist discourses reinscribe white supremacy's claims that Black culture and experience are its own.[74]

Critical, too, is the way that the historical exclusion of Black and racialized women from feminist discourse has enabled gender concepts to become ostensibly nonviolent and progressive tools of embourgeoisement. Davis documents how Black women were excluded from suffrage organizations not only because white women might withdraw but also because some advocates believed that female suffrage would hold "great advantages for white supremacy" by enlarging white political sovereignty and maintaining white dominance.[75] A similar rhetoric emerged with the white feminist crusade for birth control and reproductive rights, where "what was demanded as a 'right' for the privileged came to be interpreted as a 'duty' for the poor" women, Black people, and immigrants, and as a form of control over the populations of the marginalized.[76] By excluding Black women from the category of women and its correlates (motherhood and housewifery), the ideology of motherhood became inextricably tied to safeguarding white supremacy, and the role of the housewife became "a symbol of economic prosperity," not a symbol of gendered oppression.[77] Davis shows how feminism's main goal—and accomplishment—is the embourgeoisement of white women who further imperialist white supremacist capitalist cis-heteropatriarchy. Kimberlé Crenshaw applies the problematic of single-axis analysis of identity to both feminism and antiracism to show how "the tendency to treat race and gender as mutually exclusive categories of experience and analysis" erases the experiences of Black women.[78] While Crenshaw's critique of antidiscrimination law illustrates the need for intersectional understandings of identity to prevent that very erasure, intersectional feminism has been co-opted by white feminists to pretend to recognize its own situatedness and their relationality with other marginalized peoples. Patricia Hill Collins forecasts this co-optation: "Alternative knowledge claims in and of themselves are rarely threatening to conventional knowledge. Such claims are routinely ignored, discredited, or simply absorbed and marginalized in existing paradigms. Much more threatening is the challenge that alternative epistemologies offer to the basic process used by the powerful to legitimate their knowledge claims."[79]

This embourgeoisement of white women enables racial capitalism to erode the appearance of barriers and to redirect attention away from other forms of oppression. To emphasize white feminine vulnerability in cis-heteropatriarchy, feminism strategically casts the white woman's own (neo)liberal and racist tools as gendered sources of pain: her bitchiness, her girl squad or clique, her power couple alignment with bad men, her desire to mother, her competition with other girls and women. Much like in Taylor Swift's celebrity persona and video for "Mean," mean girl feminism justifies white women's bourgeois aspirations as gendered pathways imbued with white moral virtue. This book outlines the communication strategies, signifiers, and mechanisms that enable white women to concern themselves with heteronormative gender performance as a primary area of feminist struggle.

White Feminist Sovereignty and Agency

Since the 1970s, feminist theory has navigated the relationship between power, performativity, and the subject by developing and particularizing the concept and illustrations of agency. Saba Mahmood argues that in this post-1970s feminist framework, which analyzes participation in and subversion of patriarchal norms, agency happens thanks to the actions of an autonomous, resistant subject who defies or redeploys hegemonic practices for their "own interests and agendas."[80] In large part due to how scholars have interpreted the influential notion of performativity from Butler, agency has become coterminous with a resistance that "imposes a teleology of progressive politics." Resistant, agentic subjects seek freedom from power, whose obverse, docility, is the annulment of agency. A consequence of synonymizing agency and resistance is that it "makes it hard for us to see and understand forms of being and action that are not necessarily encapsulated by the narrative of subversion and inscription of norms."[81] Mahmood explains that the binary of resistance and subordination makes it difficult to imagine how discourses of resistance can contest strict feminine behavior norms while entrenching women in other matrixes of power. I want to further explore how a post-1970s feminist framework focused on performativity imagines agency—or what Mahmood defines as the "capacity for action that specific relations of *subordination* create and enable"—with an autonomous, resistant subject: the white cis-heterosexual woman who stylizes colonial objectives with feminism.[82]

Feminist civility is bounded by the right to be mean and rebellious under the white heteromasculine gaze. With the performative turn, feminism has become about protecting the individualized ways in which white womanhood is performed, with no obligation to or regard for how white womanhood supports other forms of oppression and without concern for social context, prevailing stereotypes, or the harmful effects of one's own actions. Feminist civility deploys identity as a wound for white women to name the problem and the solution in their lives as based on gender, in ways that ignore how identity is not reducible to gender.

This book is organized around four different terms that widen white women's performativity by disciplining civility into networks of white affection: the contestation around the label *Bitch*, most famously prompted by *The Bitch Manifesto* (chapter 1); the bifurcation of feminism and *postfeminism* (chapter 2); the emergence of the *power couple* (chapter 3); and conservative women's identity as *feminist* (chapter 4). These terms interest me because they are also terms I have been encouraged to use to create my own ethical distinction and status, but here I problematize them as tools of weaponization. Each term demonstrates how white feminism enacts embourgeoisement and "settler moves to innocence," or strategies that "problematically attempt to reconcile settler guilt and complicity, and rescue settler futurity."[83] These moves to innocence are both settler and feminist in that they normalize the range of feminine performances as consequential for a feminist futurity that evades white colonial responsibility and keeps collective freedom and liberation at bay. If whiteness as a phenomenology puts things into reach (a là Ahmed), then feminist civility inflected by whiteness puts meanness within reach as a normalized affect that can be expressed without social death.[84] As a white phenomenology, feminist civility can appear resistant to cis-heteropatriarchy, without losing everything in that resistance.

Resistance as agency is a tried and true topic of gender studies and feminist discourses, and the term *Bitch* has been theorized as feminist defiance of historical and contemporary depictions of womanhood. "Bitch Feminism: Blackfaced Girlboss in Feminist Performative/Performativity Politics" (chapter 1) explores how white recuperations of Bitch perpetuate anti-Blackness and how the worlding of feminism through Bitch performativity makes gender analysis intelligible through an entrenchment of imperialist white supremacist capitalist cis-heteropatriarchy. This chapter looks at three key examples of Bitch performativity: *The Bitch Manifesto*, written in 1968 by Joreen (Jo Freeman); the viral parody video "Bitchy Resting Face" (2013); and the boss bitch character in the comedy series *Great News* (2017–18), coproduced by Tina Fey. These texts argue that *Bitch* should be reclaimed because those who have been labeled "bitch" refuse to be "enslaved"; they are meaner and smarter than women who have submitted to Womanhood. Based on my reading of Joreen's enslavism as inspired by her envy of Black women involved in the civil rights movement, as well as the ways in which Blackness is deployed as a strategy of coolness in "Bitchy Resting Face" and *Great News*, I explore how the resignification politics of *Bitch* is a form of blackface that mimes a disempowered, resistant performativity while also refusing the legitimacy of Black people. I argue that the white bitch of Bitch feminism is invented as a better master because she can bitch her way through cis-heteropatriarchy by being the master himself as herself.

In addition to celebrating the mean girl figure for her resistant potential, feminism also positions the mean girl figure as a Trojan horse to concretize the need for an antagonistic relationship between feminism and cis-heteropatriarchy. The mean girl figure embodies racialized anger but is inarticulate about what to do post-patriarchy. "Mean Girl Feminism: Gatekeeping as Illegible Rage" (chapter 2) explores the way that rage and meanness shape feminism in media scholarship, with particular attention on the mean girl trope in the movie *Mean Girls* (2004). I examine how mean girls and women are seen as postfeminists hindering the political advancement of feminism by rendering female solidarity unlikely and caring most about subjecting themselves and others to the heteronormative masculine gaze. The solutions to mean girls put forward by feminism and its postfeminist deviations are one and the same: to locate productive outlets for releasing white women's rage by reorienting one's identity to feminist principles that source oppression to gender. In probing how the relationship between feminism and postfeminism follows the Derridean logic of the supplement, I argue that feminism's charge against postfeminism cleaves and creates a delay in feminism's arrival by reiterating itself as generating distinct social and political desires and outcomes. To distinguish feminism from postfeminism, feminist scholarship also deploys the mean girl trope, producing a binary of white mean girls (postfeminist scapegoats who render feminist conversation impossible) and white nice girls (civil, polite feminists who are prevented from articulating a feminist politic). By positioning themselves outside the logic of meanness, white nice girl feminists, like Cady from the movie *Mean Girls*, are figured as the better masters because they are not the origin of meanness, even though they inaugurate (and expose) it.

The "power couple" construction domesticates women into supportive ladies of their husbands by taking the strategies and feelings of working in community and directing these toward building a like-minded squad, coupledom, and family. As a result, power couple feminism encourages not just her individual success but their success as a cis-hetero couple. Through an analysis of recent media texts that involve the romantic endeavors of mean girls and women, "Power Couple Feminism: Gaslighting and Re-Empowering Heteronormative Aggression" (chapter 3) considers how white heterosexual love is constructed as a feminist realm that can redeem white people. The phrase *power couple* marks feminism's beneficial effects on white heterosexual marital arrangements. I argue that power couple feminism protects violent men and obscures the violence of imperialist white supremacist capitalist cis-heteropatriarchy in order to show a feminist balance of work-life. In power couple feminism, violent white men appear lovable and mean white women are redeemed as their saviors. Loving white aggressive masculinity, white mean girls are not absent of or relieved from ethical judgment, for their ethics precisely consist of upholding white heteronormative family values. The power couple feminist is a better kind of master because she claims to manage white male violence with her love.

With the popularization of gender equity, feminism has become a part of institutions interested in legitimating their power and policies with experts and administrators who are now part of the bureaucratic operations. As Raka Shome explains of global motherhood, "White femininity works for the nation as long as it can be put in the service of certain national hegemonies."[85] "Global Mother Feminism: Gatekeeping Biopower and Sovereignty" (chapter 4) examines how politically conservative women perform global motherhood in ways that are seen as compatible with liberal feminist values and commitments. Concerned more with white women's entry into politics and less with the effects of their politics on people of color, liberal feminists argued that First Lady Laura Bush and vice presidential candidate Sarah Palin too were feminists, scaffolding this argument on the white feminist values in Bush's advocacy of the American occupation of Afghanistan, and on the gendered and sexist scrutiny Palin faced in the media. I select Bush for her mild, nice demeanor and Palin for her reputation as a politically charged mean girl in order to demonstrate how popular feminism has shifted away from political prescription and toward performativity politics embodied by global motherhood. This chapter argues that feminism minimizes its antagonism toward white politically conservative women to ease political embourgeoisement and retain the capacity to determine care and quality of life in statecraft. The global mother feminist is a better master because she embeds white biopower with gendered interest and inclusion.

By focusing on gendered performance as a struggle and expanding the range of white hetero-feminine performativity as feminist, feminism effaces its own violence as a form of civility that toys with cis-heteropatriarchy and reaffirms colonial sovereignty. In the book's conclusion, "Abolishing Mean Girl Feminism," I look at various examples of meanness by racialized women to illustrate how racialized meanness operates differently in popular culture. I consider a decolonial and postcolonial form of feminism that challenges the politics of civility.

My hope for this book is not to do away with the project of feminism writ large, but instead to examine the performative turn that fosters meanness as an affective form of colonial sovereignty. Like Claudia in *The Bluest Eye*—whom Ahmed describes as a Black feminist killjoy who "uses the gift [of a white baby doll] to generate counterknowledge"—I want to use the gift of feminism to generate new understandings of how white feminism deploys itself as a form of resistance that shuts out women of color even while claiming to include them.[86] This double move is anecdotally familiar but is not yet analytically examined as emerging from feminism itself.

By exploring how feminism establishes the mean white woman protagonist as both a patriarchal problem and a nonviolent sign of progress, this book shows how performativity screens the insecurity and precarity around white feminist politics of recognition. Mean girl feminism reduces the oppression of cis-heteropatriarchy into communicative interactions and performatives that are within the articulate feminist's control and ease. Normalizing confrontations with sexism in this way prevents robust engagement with the intersection of patriarchal oppression and other systems of power. The performative turn serves not only neoliberal ends (where subjects value authenticity and free self-expression as a hallmark of successfully resisting power) but also colonial interests (dispersing violence onto subjects that have reflected inward about gender oppression and externalized their rebellion interpersonally, without direction and without fault). Turning to performativity—how to act, what to wear, how to comport oneself—allows feminism to realign itself as disrupting cis-heteropatriarchy rather than imagine new forms of collective freedom. Feminist civility gaslights people of color, gatekeeps anger, and girlbosses a future that holds a special place for white women in cis-heteropatriarchy, when that anger could otherwise be sublimated into collective liberation.

CHAPTER 1

BITCH FEMINISM

Blackfaced Girlboss in Feminist Performative/Performativity Politics

In a July 2020 speech addressing the US House, Representative Alexandria Ocasio-Cortez (D-NY) described a heated exchange with Representative Ted Yoho (R-FL) in which Yoho called her "a fucking bitch" for her views on poverty and crime. In speaking out about the incident, Ocasio-Cortez suggested that it was the racialized and classed context of her background and politics that incited Yoho's sexist slur. Ocasio-Cortez's speech articulates the intended pain and the rhetorical force of the word, as well as the way white patriarchal values continue to structure the regime of power that she firmly opposes. In effect, Ocasio-Cortez underscores the material harm that conditions the lived experience of racialized women, a kind of wound that cannot be redirected to feminist identity and intentionality. In her speech and her follow-up tweet that "'b*tches' get stuff done," Ocasio-Cortez does not reclaim the term *bitch* and does not rationalize Bitch performativity as cause for her success or motivation for being.

In feminist discourses, Bitch signifies the potential range of women's performativity as an important challenge to patriarchal power. The word emblazoned the cover of a popular feminist magazine, in circulation from 1996 through 2022, which reappropriated the term as its title in honor of women "who speak their minds, who have opinions and don't shy away from expressing them, and who don't sit by and smile uncomfortably if they're bothered or offended."[1] However differently, Black women rappers have long been reclaiming or challenging the use of the term by men, from Queen Latifah's "U.N.I.T.Y." (1993) and Lil' Kim's "Queen Bitch" (1996) to Young M.A's "Bad Bitch Anthem" (2020). For many scholars in gender studies, the long history of negatively representing women characters in books and media represents the danger women's agency poses to cis-heteropatriarchy; they turn to Bitch as a nodal point of womanhood that opposes this cis-heteropatriarchy. Focusing on the 1990s media amid the prominent challenges posed by Anita Hill (with her testimony against Supreme Court nominee Clarence Thomas) and others, Allison Yarrow tracks the heterosexist backlash and construction of women into bitches as "bitchification."[2] In her exhaustive study of the bitch character in Western literature, Sarah Appleton Aguiar argues that feminism, all too caught up in positive representations of women, should affirm its antipatriarchal power to liberate women subjects from the performative constraints of traditional womanhood.[3] An anthem for many white feminists, guitarist Meredith Brooks's song "Bitch" (1997) puts Bitch feminism succinctly in its lyrics: "So take me as I am / This may mean you'll have to be a stronger man." Kalene Westmoreland discusses how this song and the contemporaneous music festival Lilith Fair helped "turn suffering into an affirmation: a kind of strength through vulnerability."[4] For white feminism, bitch/Bitch holds the communicative convenience of calling attention to cis-heteropatriarchy as a system that genders and discriminates against women as a category, and, at the same time, indicating resistant intentionality about women's performativity.

The above literature and examples prompt me to explore the extent to which Bitch is the postmodern mark of white feminist maturity and sovereignty—or the embodiment of "fourth wave white feminism," as Koa Beck writes.[5] In 2021, the TikTok fake cry challenge involved white women showing how convincing they can pretend to cry. In the viral video from Hannah Stocking (@hannahstocking) that started the trend, her tears are put into question by an ironic smirk that suggests white women's knowledge and manipulation of performative power. I wonder about the ways in which Bitch aligns feminism with white patriarchal structures and norms through an inflated array of performances that do not question the terms and conditions of sovereign power itself. In this chapter, I ask: What if bitchiness is just mean? In what ways is one performing gender or feminism when one is bitchy? How do the reclamation politics of Bitch construct meanness as feminist and not antiracist? As I demonstrate, the discourse of reclaiming Bitch illustrates how meanness normalizes resistance as the performativity of white women in ways not granted to other populations. Feminist resistance relies on a politically motivated interiority and intentionality as the source of white feminine goodness and virtue. Bitch performativity enables white women to construct womanhood and even retroactively rationalize and politicize their meanness as feminist.

Echoing Audre Lorde, who wisely insisted that Black feminism is not white feminism in blackface, I argue that white feminism is in fact equity in blackface.[6] White feminism operates in blackface through the performative and performativity of Bitch. If iterations of blackface can happen in the miming of Black performances, without the utterance of Black English(es) or the darkening of white faces, then the feminist reclamation of Bitch encourages white women to mime the defiant mannerisms, attitudes, and styles of Black women. In Kyla Schuller's words, "White feminism is theft disguised as liberation."[7] Putting Black women's performativity under erasure, feminist reclamations of Bitch stage a "love and theft," to borrow a phrase from Eric Lott, of Black women, breaking the color line only to perform aspects of Black womanhood with resistant flair and heteronormative flirt.[8] Feminism gatekeeps the category of women, leaving women of color as mere feminine or femme types whose performativity can be appropriated for Woman. Bitch feminism steals the clapback of the angry Black woman, the resting bitch face of the dragon lady, the expressiveness of the upset Latinx, and the refusal of the unyielding Indigenous woman, and appropriates their tactics as white feminist rebellion.[9] Bitch feminism regenerates white womanhood as a progressive and intentional site of feminism.

Drawing from Eric Lott and Patricia Hill Collins, this chapter discusses blackface as a performance that provokes both fear and fascination of Blackness, and I trace the racial history that informs the terms and performativity of Bitch/bitch. I turn to the popularly cited 1968/70 *The Bitch Manifesto* by Joreen (Jo Freeman), which conceives gender performance as either compliant with womanhood or deviant to patriarchal power. I show that Bitch feminism constructs gender performance as problematically situated within patriarchal power, but can become an intentional act of resistance. In order to tie gender performativity to feminist intention, Joreen sediments womanhood to sexism, and Bitch to feminism, thereby abstracting gender performativity from their racialized contexts. I also analyze the performativity of Bitch in popular culture as feminist blackface by considering Broken People's viral parody video "Bitchy Resting Face" (2013), as well as Tina Fey's comedy series *Great News* (2017–18), which features Fey as the "Boardroom Bitch." Both texts demonstrate how Bitch performativity operates by disavowing the knowledge that the Bitch figure has white prestige and does not name and contextualize the intersecting systems of oppression. I argue that Bitch feminism encourages its targeted white woman to perform bitchiness as an effaced Black womanhood in order to demonstrate herself as a sovereign. The Bitch feminist is capable of being the master himself—now as herself.

Blackfacing Feminism through Resignifying Bitch

In common parlance, blackface has been used to describe when people darken their face in order to represent themselves as Black. But blackface involves more than just makeup: it is a well-worn convention of North American culture that involves the performance act of donning qualities and characteristics of Blackness. Dating back to the American antebellum period, the minstrel show helped set up racial distinctions between white and non-white peoples through skin color by featuring white actors in blackface who mimed stereotypical Blackness to appeal to white audiences. In his study of minstrel theater during the 1820s to 1850s, Eric Lott analyzes how blackface minstrelsy was a screen on which white working-class audiences projected their class and racial anxieties. According to Lott, blackface played out racial ambivalence and a simultaneous dialectic of attraction and repulsion for the racialized other. Behind the racist hatred and revulsion was also a desire for the features of Blackness, which were seen by working-class white people as insurrectionary, to forge class politics and conflict against the white bourgeoisie. Although some minstrel shows deliberated on abolitionism and other racial reforms, the theatrical functions of blackface were less about staging identification and sympathy with Black people, and more about offering up representations through which white audiences could explore their own white identity in contestation of class demarcation. Blackface's legacy, too, is found in the familiar racist stereotypes of redface and brownface evident in American sports and movies and Canadian mainstream media. Such tropes are often justified on the grounds that they retain the buying potential of white viewership for advertisers, leading Daniel Morley Johnson to coin the term "whitestream media."[10] White celebrities like Iggy Azalea, Ariana Grande, Calvin Harris, Rita Ora, and the Kardashian/Jenner family have undergone aesthetic transformations known as *blackfishing*, a term created by Wanna Thompson to refer to strategies that promote racial ambiguity or suggestion: tanning, darkening their photos on Instagram, changing their names, and undergoing plastic surgery. Like the minstrel show, blackfishing is intended not so much to attract non-white audiences, but to appeal to more white liberal audience members who want to diversify and add "spice" to their life.[11] As W. T. Lhamon writes, "blackface fascination shows a miscegenated culture becoming aware of itself."[12] Thus, the practices of blackface, blackfishing, and white exotification are symptomatic of whitestream media and culture—including feminism—recognizing racial tensions by appropriating Black and racialized muses for a rebellious, cool aesthetic.

Black images, characters, and representations, albeit mostly of the negative kind, proliferate in popular culture and media. For working-class Black women, according to Patricia Hill Collins, there are two main assemblages of representations: *bitch* and *Bitch*. Bitches with the lowercase *b* are Black women who are "aggressive, loud, rude, and pushy." Applied to poor and working-class Black women, this label "constitutes a reworking of the image of the mule of chattel slavery," which functioned as a foil to the aggression ascribed to Black women. While any Black woman can be a bitch, Bitches with the capital *B* are Black women who are "super-tough, super-strong women who are often celebrated." Collins describes early 1970s films that featured Black women who put their "looks, sexuality, intellect, and/or aggression in service of African American communities."[13] Pam Grier's characters in *Sheba, Baby* (1975) and *Foxy Brown* (1974) were Black women who used beauty, sexuality, and violence to challenge the status quo and improve their communities. However, garnering as much criticism as praise, Grier's characters illustrate how "Black female strength is depicted and then stigmatized."[14] Here, too, within the term *bitch* itself—delicately altered by a mere capital letter—Collins notices the dialectical dance of envy and insult toward Blackness and Black women that has long been part of the racialized scene staged by whitestream media.

Considered a foundational text in the late 1960s and 1970s women's liberation movement and a current mainstay in popular feminist consciousness, *The Bitch Manifesto* was one of the first texts to attempt to transform the meaning of a slur, a rhetorical process known as language reclamation or resignification.[15] Written by feminist organizer and activist Joreen (Jo Freeman) in 1968, *The Bitch Manifesto* argues that *Bitch* is a term slung at women who do not perform traditional submissive femininity. Joreen's Bitch is capitalized and is taken directly, without attribution, from Black women who are her source of inspiration. Embodying and expressing total agency and sovereignty, a Bitch's aggressive performativity is, according to Joreen, a consequence of refusing cis-heteropatriarchy's notions of womanhood. My analysis of Joreen's inspiration (which she would detail years later in the 1995 document *On the Origins of the Women's Liberation Movement from a Strictly Personal Perspective*) and *The Bitch Manifesto* reveals that the feminist resignification of the term *Bitch* is founded on an enslavism that situates the undervalued qualities associated with women as slave characteristics. Enslavism appropriates the conditions and language of slavery to make arguments about feminist progress and render Woman as oppressed by cis-heteropatriarchy.[16] *The Bitch Manifesto* suggests that the white feminist is a better master because she recognizes cis-heteropatriarchy as a form of oppression that is akin to slavery. By treating slavery as a metaphor of its oppression, feminism produces a notion of white womanhood that simultaneously is mean enough to undergird white supremacy (she is a Bitch) and, at the same time, nice or innocent enough to excuse white women from it (she is Woman). To write *The Bitch Manifesto*, Joreen distilled the characteristics of Black women with whom she worked during the civil rights movement as "Bitch" feminist qualities to admire and emulate. Feminism in *The Bitch Manifesto* becomes a mode of performativity that frees white "Bitchy" women from the enslaved subjection that they never had.

Over the course of *On the Origins of the Women's Liberation Movement*, it becomes clear that *The Bitch Manifesto* was inspired by Joreen's participation in the civil rights movement, which she credits for rousing her interest in gender equality. Much like how abolitionism helped give white women a "grounding in early feminism,"[17] Joreen admits that her activism in the civil rights movement was less about ensuring racial justice, and more about furthering her own self-interest, gaining knowledge and experience in advocating for equity:

> Learning that this movement had been the incubator for the woman's rights movement, and seeing the parallels between that time and my own, led me to speculate that the next major movement would be one of women. I didn't tell anyone, because I knew everyone would laugh at me, but I did tuck it into the back of my mind as something to look for. "Women" also became a subtext for my reading about black Americans and the social and psychological consequences of racism. I looked around and applied what I learned by analogy. This in turn forced me to confront my own very real prejudices about women.[18]

In discussing her role and experience with the Southern Christian Leadership Conference (SCLC)—the Black civil rights organization first led by Dr. Martin Luther King Jr.—Joreen discredits Black people's relation to equity ("laugh at me") and focuses on the harassment women staff members were subjected to. As if her experience was a wound, she omits mention of the racist practices and institutions that led to the civil rights protests and the strategies of SCLC, and instead describes her participation as an analogical tool to develop an understanding of equity from which to found her own feminist program and politics. Even when her role puts her at risk, making her a public target of white supremacist hate, the lessons Joreen gained from the civil rights movement provided little insight into her own racial performance or the racializing structures that brought about the need for the movement in the first place. In *On the Origins of the Women's Liberation Movement*, she repeats anti-intersectional scenarios in which race opposes gender in ways that mirror the racism of white suffragettes from an earlier era: she is infuriated by a young man receiving the floor to speak on American

Indians at the National Conference for New Politics; she observes that the civil rights movement centrally shaped her thinking but failed to give her "contacts with minority women"; and she questions whether "a respectable black female political scientist" and author (who is not named but is likely Linda La Rue) fully realized the implications of her magazine article title "Black Liberation and Woman's Lib."[19] Over and over in her reflections on the women's liberation movement, Joreen discusses her involvement in the civil rights movement as a gateway for developing gender consciousness.

Joreen segues from her irritations as a civil rights participant observer to the difference Black women made within movement activities, which "nudged [her] in the feminist direction." She explains,

> Black women seemed different from white women. They seemed stronger, and more importantly, that strength was accepted, not denigrated. They occupied more social space, played more roles, were a bigger presence in their communities than I had seen white women occupy. None fit the "clinging vine" stereotype popular at the time or seemed to want to. Some of the subconscious contempt in which I had always held women because of this "feminine ideal" began to melt away. The Black women I saw and worked with provided a different model of how to be a woman in our society, and the Black community displayed a different attitude toward strong women. This opened a whole realm of possibilities.[20]

Her description of Black women's strength parallels much of the language found in *The Bitch Manifesto* that enables her to transform the negative valence on women's aggression into a positive performativity that actualizes the feminist self: "A Bitch occupies a lot of psychological space. . . . One of the sources of their suffering as women is also a source of their strength."[21] Similarities between her reflections on the civil rights movement and *The Bitch Manifesto* are evident, too, in the part of *On the Origins of the Women's Liberation Movement* where she recounts working for Coretta Scott King:

> During the six weeks I worked for her my admiration grew. She was much more than a minister's wife and mother. Her personal ambitions and concerns had been stifled by Dr. King's prominence and the need to play her part in the Civil Rights Movement, but they had not been lost; she had plans to move on her own interests when times were less intense. Before I left, my growing admiration led to another feminist "click." I realized that I was 21 years old, and she was the first woman I had ever met that I truly admired.[22]

It is no surprise, then, that Joreen portrays a Bitch as a woman who "will often espouse contentment with being the power behind the throne—provided that she does have real power—while rationalizing that she really does not want the recognition that comes with also having the throne."[23] Given all the talk from Joreen about the significant impact of Black women on her feminist consciousness, one would imagine that *The Bitch Manifesto* would give similar credit to Black women. But, nowhere in *The Bitch Manifesto* does Joreen offer credit to the Black women whom she admired and envied.

If *On the Origins of the Women's Liberation Movement* illustrates how Black women are Joreen's inspiration to write about Bitch performativity as feminism, then *The Bitch Manifesto* is evidence of how that source of inspiration is erased. Metaphor is a colonial strategy to destroy or assimilate the other, as Eve Tuck and K. Wayne Yang argue, and resistant leftist politics can be fraught with white settlers who try to become other instead of recognizing their own role in colonial erasure.[24] Similarly, Sabine Broeck writes of feminism's deployment of analogy and metaphor: "White feminism, to which gender theory is still and again indebted, has been a discourse of negative analogy—We are not slaves, we are not property!—ranging from Wollstonecraft through Simone de Beauvoir to second- and third-wave feminism, and not stopping there."[25] Joreen begins *The Bitch Manifesto* with an epigraph from Beauvoir that emphasizes how women's human (rather than feminine) qualities are grounds to be "accused of trying to emulate the male." Similar to Beauvoir, who sought "to enter woman into philosophy"—a quest that hinged on "her idea of the woman being enslaved by her body or, more precisely, by her reproductive function"—Joreen positions a specific kind of woman as a worthy antagonist to man.[26] Whereas the enslaved subject for Beauvoir is woman's negative ideal, intended to illustrate woman's capability as equal to that of man, the woman as enslaved subject for Joreen is the Bitch's negative counterpoint, intended to magnify the inferiority of womanhood. To reject the qualities of womanhood, Joreen treats the woman as slave as a negative metaphor for *both* whom/what man is not and whom/what a Bitch is not. Underutilized and objectified, and not living up to her potential, the woman as slave works for men, ignorantly aims for amicability, and follows rules and norms. Joreen contrasts woman with Bitch, who refuses to play by those same rules: "For this resistance [Bitches] were roundly condemned. They were put down, snubbed, sneered at, talked about, laughed at, and ostracized. Our society made women into slaves and then condemned them for acting like slaves."[27] This analogy ("acting like slaves") becomes a metaphor: women become "slaves" when they accept their objectification. Abstracted of the lived experience and material conditions of white enslavement of Black peoples, slavery is figured here as feminine submissiveness, whose metaphorical shackles and chains can be broken with a sharp wit and tongue, a large physical and emotional presence, and independent decision-making.

Joreen infuses Bitch feminism with an otherness of which it is not. Joreen blackfaces gendered dispossession by appropriating characteristics of Black womanhood and enslavement in order to theorize Bitch feminism as a progressive foil to white womanhood. Her language conjures the conditions and experiences of Black women in the Americas during the transatlantic slave trade and its afterlife, as she writes that a Bitch is "a special category created [by men] in which she is accounted at least partially human, but not really a woman. . . . Women are even more threatened because they cannot forget she is a woman. They are afraid they will identify with her too closely. She has a freedom and an independence which they envy and challenges them to forsake the security of their chains." Beneath both men and women in the social hierarchy and immune to the white notions of "proper sex role behavior," a Bitch is the partial human whose "chains" were never cause for "security."[28] As the independent and free third figure of the man-woman binary (where woman is enslaved and "chained" to man), a Bitch is the (Black) woman who refused to cater to (white) man's wishes and desires, and whose features of Black womanhood are appropriated to express indifference to the white male gaze. Joreen writes, "They are subjects, not objects. They may have a relationship with a person or organization, but they never marry anyone or anything; man, mansion, or movement. Thus, Bitches prefer to plan their own lives rather than live from day to day, action to action, or person to person."[29] For Joreen, the Bitch thrives (in her liberation in the afterlife of slavery) in ways that (white) womanhood does not.

The Bitch Manifesto proposes that cis-heteropatriarchy's agon is the Bitch who refuses to exhibit characteristics attributed to slavery. By reading white feminism as a form of blackface and as an act of both "love and theft," I have shown that The Bitch Manifesto is a tool or a technology of the self that transforms embourgeoisement into moral performances of gender. The resignification of Bitch is not simply a feminist mode of pushing back against the patriarchal strictures of womanhood; it is a disavowal of the violence of white women's aggression, a disavowal that positions that aggression as feminist. Through this figuration, The Bitch Manifesto creates a white feminist superiority complex that can be projected onto white women's mean performativity. Most harmfully, The Bitch Manifesto encourages a lack of care about women's positionality inside institutional structures, a lack of care that ultimately reinforces her own whiteness.

While *The Bitch Manifesto* lays out the principles for utilizing *Bitch* as a term of gendered empowerment and embracing associated characteristics for white feminist expression, white women's cross-racial uses of the term do not stray far from the racialized history of *The Bitch Manifesto*. *Bitch* as a term became a major source of contention on *The Real Housewives of Atlanta* (2008–), when Kim Zolciak, the only white woman on the reality television show, regularly called her Black employee, Sweetie, the epithet in front of the Black women cast members, who found it racist and unacceptable. Historically, white women slung the epithet at mixed-race enslaved women in the "fancy trade," where white men purchased sexual slaves. If, as Stephanie Jones-Rogers has argued, the history of white women as impassioned, if not capable, slave masters has been suppressed, then Bitch feminism reconstructs the logic of the female master as that of the feminist resister.[30] Reclaiming Bitch brings about a racializing assemblage that "upgrades" white feminism and facilitates the erasure of Black and racial knowledge and life. Alexander Weheliye explains the problems in reform and inclusion: "Where dominant discourse seeks to develop upgrades of the current notions of humanity as Man, improvements are not the aim or product of the imaginaries borne of racializing assemblages and political violence; instead they summon forms of human emancipation that can be imagined but not (yet) described."[31]

Blackfacing the Performativity of the Girlboss

Having established that Joreen's recuperation of Bitch as feminist performativity seizes and erases aspects of Black womanhood, I turn in this section to how Bitch feminism constructs white women in neoliberalism as girlbosses capable of sovereign power and even as sovereignty's best agents. I begin with the phenomenon known as "resting bitch face" (RBF), specifically as it is taken up in the medical parody video "Bitchy Resting Face" from Broken People. RBF is a celebrated performance of Bitch feminism that ascribes white interiority and intentionality to untraditional femininity. As Bitch feminism, RBF puts forward a mean facade that codes and coalesces feminist civility rather than actualizing protest. In performing RBF, the Bitch feminist assumes that her interiority protects her intentionality to be and do differently gender performance. But, Bitch performativity tries on Black womanhood and performs it with feminist intention that is denied to Black women. Then, I examine Tina Fey's *Great News*, where Fey herself appears as the "Boardroom Bitch," to illustrate how feminist blackface does not require the literal blackening of white faces to detach Blackness from race, and how feminist blackface maps its cultural referents onto a neoliberal trajectory to create gender equity between white men and white women.

Popularized in 2013, the term *resting bitch face* describes a face that, when at rest, looks mean, aggressive, or otherwise unapproachable. RBF is a label usually targeted at women who do not conform to the societal expectations that they regularly smile and get along with others. In the spoof public service announcement "Bitchy Resting Face" (2013), which was created by Broken People (the comedy project of writer-comedian Taylor Orci and her then boyfriend) and posted to the website *Funny or Die*, RBF is caricatured as an underlying health condition that many women unknowingly have, where their face does not reflect their personality or intention. Parodying medical infomercials, the video, which quickly went viral, shows confessionals from white women who say that they too have "bitchy resting face," followed by a montage of various interactions: with their white male partner as he discusses his devotion, with a Black woman cashier as they complete a transaction, and with their white male partner as he proposes on bended knee. While their grimaces, side-eyes, and furrowed eyebrows are seen as unintentional to their male partners, the cold interaction with the Black woman cashier stands out because the white woman offers no explanation or apology and the Black woman is visibly and audibly upset by her meanness, yelling "ok?!" In the second half of the video, a series of white men confess that they have "resting asshole face" and experience the same social confusion between their facial expression and their interior feeling. Together, the white people request that viewers not judge or label their personalities based on their faces. When Taylor, one of the confessing women and also the producer, rationalizes, "If we wanted to be constantly misunderstood, we'd try to talk to a deaf person," the surrounding group calls Taylor a bitch. After her retort that they should have been aborted, one woman shouts "Bitch" back at Taylor. The pseudo-medical infomercial challenges the expectation that women should smile by illustrating how Bitch functions as both a performative and a performativity that is central to the feminist project of renegotiating the interpretation of white women.[32]

While calling attention to the term's intended pain, the medical parody suggests an interior virtue that underlies white women's facial and audible expressions. RBF is predicated on the withholding of white feminine affection as a form of regulation, as a way of managing power relations through the means of disavowed control: her face. White women's performativity becomes structurally ambiguous and frustrating to interpret because it is projected as a form of feminist service and activism, regardless of its very content or direction. White women perform RBF, miming the facial expressions and attitude of the Black woman cashier in advance of denying recognition of the cashier's very personhood. The misalignment between white women's nonverbal communication and its interpretation is ignored. The contradiction is smoothed over with feminist demands of an empathetic ethos, which also is extended to white men with "resting asshole face." White women may have RBF, but they still love and empathize with their white men partners, reiterating their commitment to white cis-heteronormativity.

It is worth repeating Sara Ahmed's warning about the relationship between feminism and willfulness. She cautions that we must "not reduce willfulness to againstness. There is a family of words around willfulness (*stubborn, obstinate, defiant, rude, reckless*), which creates a structure of resemblance (we feel we know what she is like). This familialism also explains how easily willfulness is confused with, and reduced to, individualism. We need to resist this reduction. The reduction is how willful subjects are dismissed."[33] It is this reduction—which is introduced without engagement with racial embodiment—that is central to Bitch performativity.

The affective worlding of feminism through Bitch performativity is depicted through much of comedian Tina Fey's work. Becoming well known in *Saturday Night Live* (where she was head writer in 1999–2006), Fey has established herself as a writer, producer, and actor in television and film. From successful television series *30 Rock* (2006–13) and *Unbreakable Kimmy Schmidt* (2015–20) to movie hits *Mean Girls* (2004; which I analyze in chapter 2) and *Baby Mama* (2008), Fey's writing as an act of feminist control has been lauded as groundbreaking for women, garnering several Golden Globes, Writers Guild Awards, and many other accolades. *Great News* (2017–18), on which she also guest stars in the second season, is one of her more recent productions. Set behind the scenes at the fictional cable news network MMN and its show *The Breakdown*, *Great News* follows the news producer Katie Wendelson (played by Briga Heelan); her mother and a *Breakdown* intern, Carol (Andrea Martin); Katie's boss and love interest, Greg Walsh (Adam Campbell); and the two co-anchors, Portia Scott-Griffith (Nicole Richie) and Chuck Pierce (John Michael Higgins). In her debut episode, titled "Boardroom Bitch" (season 2, episode 1), Fey's character, Diana St. Tropez, becomes the new network president. As the announcement is made and the staff assumes the new hire to be male, Diana, undercover as a male janitor, dramatically interrupts the chatter by revealing her identity. Katie notes that Diana, an idol of hers, wrote the book *Boardroom Bitch*, and Diana enumerates the list of sacrifices she makes to be successful. Over the next few episodes, Katie seeks Diana's mentorship, much to her mother's chagrin; Diana and Portia feud over their professional reputations; and Diana sexually harasses the men at MMN, in hopes of receiving a "golden parachute" payout of the sort that male executives have been awarded after inappropriate behavior.

Neoliberalism absorbs notions of equity by not only casting economic opportunity as the condition of possibility for realizing individual identity, but also imagining identity as reaching its full potential and capacity through the egotistical and violent character of the white man: unshakable pride, aggressive shell of invincibility, and an excess of self-confidence. Bitch feminism has turned this idea into less violent, feminist advisement that can be found in starter cross-stitching kits and art prints: "Carry Yourself with the Confidence of a Mediocre White Man." To this end, Diana might be read as a neoliberal and postfeminist figuration that Angela McRobbie would call "phallic girl," one who enacts all privileges of hegemonic masculinity but displays all the signifiers of a polished cultural womanhood.[34] Diana embraces the characteristics associated with toxic masculinity to reach her full potential as a leader: arrogance, aggression, and invulnerability. Much like other girlboss characters—such as Miranda Priestly (Meryl Streep) in *The Devil Wears Prada* (2006), Jane Smith (Angelina Jolie) in *Mr. & Mrs. Smith* (2005), and Penny Rust (Rebel Wilson) and Josephine Chesterfield (Anne Hathaway) in *The Hustle* (2019)—Diana performs the stereotype of bitch as the obverse of womanhood: pushing men out of her way, choosing to not help potential protégés, deeming herself too important to arrive on time, and fully investing in her own self-advancement. The role that Diana's womanhood plays helps the male characters feel comfortable about her leadership. However, to categorize the phallic girl's gender performance as a display of untraditional womanhood and masculine characteristics reinscribes and reduces women's performativity to aspects of the sex binary. McRobbie's phallic girl analysis would overemphasize gender as a category.

At another level, if we read Diana as Bitch feminism, *Great News* demonstrates the very problems arising from performativity's integration of white feminist politics. While Diana is depicted as an intentional feminist in her every movement, speech act, and expression, her Bitch performativity is tempered by the awkwardness of both Katie's lack of self-confidence and Carol's traditional maternal womanhood. The playful comparison between Diana and Carol—with Katie wanting to be like Diana and respectfully distance herself from her mother—posits Diana's business acumen and dedication as feminist performativity that politicizes neoliberal advancement as an ethical alternative to motherhood. Where Carol seems to put her needs after everyone else's, Diana puts her needs after capitalist participation (or acts as if her needs are the same as capitalism itself). As Diana makes pronouncements about the importance of freezing eggs and focusing on career, her Bitch feminism constructs the drive for capital accumulation as crucial to addressing patriarchal power. The phallus that Diana wields obscures not only her neoliberal commitment, but also her very racialization as a white woman. Diana willingly accepts the inhumane working conditions of capitalism under the progressive banner of feminism in order to demonstrate white women's superior efficiency and effectivity at enforcing the master's logic. It is through her whiteness that she can demand that she be treated the same as the sexually harassing men who leave rich(er), but it is through her gender that the MMN staff ignore her sexual harassment and accept her violence as feminist rationality: intentional and equitable. Indeed, her sexual harassment is minimized to assert feminism's deferral and continued need. As a girlboss, she is better than men who lose out on her unrealized potential due to their sexism, and she is better than other women who are caught up in negative perceptions of womanhood.

Where feminist scholars argue that feminism demands gender equity, I see feminism's demands as creating sameness among white people. Feminism has turned the phallus and the phallic girl that is Diana into another white object of fascination, where her specific embodiment of feminist performativity is the reason for surveillance or public interest. Katie's curiosity in how Diana creates work-life balance is a projection of her own aspiration to become bourgeois, a desire that casts gender as a pathway for white moral virtue and advancement. Although Diana notes her many sacrifices and efforts at self-care, her body and personal life are bereft of toll and toil.[35] Her flawlessness points to a white feminine interiority that seems good and principled for the superior role of network president. That is, gender may have contributed to Diana's struggle, but it remains on the periphery. While feminist scholars might see gender on the periphery as postfeminist, I consider this periphery to be an important constitutive site for generating feminist sensibility. With Diana having transformed herself into a sovereign subject perfect for neoliberalism, her reversal of the sex binary does not deploy the language and logic of empowerment, where the weak are lifted up by the strong. Diana chooses a deferred politics and pleasure that is arrived at when she is recognized as equal to successful white men.

Contrasted to Diana's Bitch feminism, which Katie seeks out for her own neoliberal advancement, is Portia's gauche deployment of aesthetics, optics, and millennial language. Played by Nicole Richie, Portia's character imports Richie's self-described "half-Black" background, rendering her performance racially ambiguous, at best. On the one hand, Portia is depicted as having many stereotypical "blonde" moments (she is self-involved and worried about self-presentation, an expert at whitestream celebrity culture), but on the other hand, Portia creates and dances in a hip-hop music video with a girl squad and regularly articulates complex observations in highly technical vernacular. However, her blonde, straight hair and other features of her phenotype coupled with her feminine performativity encourage viewers to see her role on *Great News* as contributing to rather than disrupting the white homogeneous setting.[36] Nevertheless, after tensions escalate between Diana and Portia, the drama culminates in Portia and Diana agreeing to monetize their feud and equally divide the profits. Portia becomes an equal peer to Diana and part of her clique, not because she is made into a CEO but because she offers knowledge and a monetizable market that Diana does not have access to.

While Portia is coded as both white and racially ambiguous, and even Diana portrays a super-tough and super-strong capacity to work, an explicit display of Blackness is not necessary to Bitch feminism. As Lott explains of the social and economic currency of blackface within white commodity culture, the resemblance between the early minstrel show and the music genres of bluegrass and rock 'n' roll is no coincidence. Although blackface once enforced the relationship between culture and race, blackface also enabled a remapping of that relationship.[37] The performance of Bitch can borrow Blackness without showing and naming it. Regarding herself as too important to respect the time of others, Diana does not need to cite "Colored People Time." Although sleeping only two hours a night, Diana does not need to problematically analogize her working conditions to slavery. She might side-eye Portia, but Diana does not need black makeup on her face. Rather than upsetting the very terms of achievement and structural oppression, the blackfaced girlboss romanticizes the grit and grind that racialized people must endure to survive, and her very achievement through that grit and grind forms the basis of her meanness and dissatisfaction with patriarchy. She girlbosses through feminism: she may vent and rant about work as unfinished feminism, so that, as the popularized feminist saying goes, "nevertheless, she persists." Bitch performativity in *Great News* brings forth the strong feeling of significance, the sharp focus of a goal, the curt tone of intelligence, and the impetus of changing the status quo, but with a deracialized lightness that comes with and through Fey's writing and acting. As Rafia Zakaria notes, "Many white women perform wokeness quite well . . . appropriating the culture of Black, Brown, or Asian people to boost their own cosmopolitan credentials."[38] The auspice of comedy and the theatrical conditions of television allow white feminism to explore Bitch performativity by detaching Bitch from Blackness, and replotting Bitch onto a neoliberal trajectory toward white, gender-neutral sameness. As Lott writes, "the blackface mask has indeed been worn as an equivocal emblem of popular resistance, on behalf, variously—even simultaneously—of tradition and innovation."[39] The pleasure of performing Bitch feminism arises in the cool, innovative, and fresh possibilities of portraying an effaced Black womanhood.

Conclusion

Feminist meanness brings white womanhood into rhetorical circulation by providing a critical texture to white women's performativity that appears different, rebellious, and unexpected against their white patriarchal kinfolk. Bitch feminism imbues white feminine performativity with moral intentionality and the feminist sophistication of antipatriarchal protest. The attempt to resignify the term *bitch* as feminist vernacular situates white women as gender conscious and gender forward. As a form of civility, Bitch feminism empowers women to think that they are singularly expressing womanhood in their performativity. *The Bitch Manifesto* offers Bitch as a figuration that white feminists can project onto their performativity. Through my analyses of "Bitchy Resting Face" and *Great News*, I demonstrated that Bitch feminism operates within a white vernacular that attempts to hail women and organize them around anti-Blackness. Drawing on a language of enslavism, omitting proper credit to Black women, and appropriating the characteristics of Blackness are the strategies white feminism uses to reconstitute Bitch as a deracialized figure of gender resistance and professional empowerment. Blackface, enslavism, and the erasure of Blackness widen feminism's allure and restage its rebellious aesthetic. Bitch feminism depends on Blackness without engaging with it, and models itself on Black experience without embodying it.

This Bitch feminism contrasts to what was expressed in Ocasio-Cortez's speech discussed at the start of this chapter. Ocasio-Cortez's work in and out of Washington is a good contemporary example of Collins's Bitch: she utilizes her embodiment and performativity to work in the service of her community. For Ocasio-Cortez, *Bitch* is not a label to revel in, and to do so would be to ground identity solely on an injury, numbing the material effects of language. The resignification of Bitch validates antipatriarchal performativity for white women without undertaking "a much deeper engagement with the architecture of the self that undergirds a particular mode of living and attachment," of which gender identity is just a part.[40] In white vernacular, resignification generates feminist meaning for white women's performativity that is structured on patriarchal inclusion, representation, and the right to be mean. In contrast, Ocasio-Cortez exposes the "architecture" of the patriarchal naming of identity and self. This engagement is essential in order to get beyond the politics of rights, recognition, or representation, and, to use the words of Saba Mahmood, to move "toward the *retraining* of ethical sensibilities so as to create a new social and moral order."[41]

The next chapter discusses mean girl feminism as a form of civility that demarcates good feminism from bad, or what is termed *postfeminism*. To construct postfeminism as antifeminist, white feminism situates women's performativity within the heteronormative male gaze, arguing that the discourse of beauty pits woman against woman, rendering feminist solidarity unlikely. Chapter 2 shows how both feminist and postfeminist discourses attempt to bypass the nice/mean girl dynamic by redirecting white feminine rage back at cis-heteropatriarchy and the category of gender. I argue that the demarcation of postfeminism by white liberal feminism is a rhetorical strategy to disavow the knowledge that postfeminism has become feminism's supplement: a corruption that has not simply been added on to "good" feminism, but has replaced it. Feminism, too, is replete with meanness that gatekeeps what is and is not feminist.

CHAPTER 2

MEAN GIRL FEMINISM
Gatekeeping as Illegible Rage

In a conversation between friends Audre Lorde and Adrienne Rich published in *Sister Outsider* (1984), Lorde discloses that she stages conversations in her head with Rich as if their individual voices function as stereotypical or symbolic subject positions: the Black lesbian and the white lesbian. Lorde recalls a real conversation where Rich demanded that Lorde provide evidence and documentation of her experience of oppression. Rich defensively says that documentation permits her to "take seriously the spaces between us that difference has created, that racism has created." Lorde suggests in turn that judging interior knowledge as insufficient evidence and treating documentation and articulation as superior knowledge are central tenets of the Western enlightenment project: "But documentation does not help one perceive. At best it only analyzes the perception. At worst, it provides a screen by which to avoid concentrating on the core revelation, following it down to how it feels. Again, knowledge and understanding. They can function in concert, but they don't replace each other." Lorde explains that requiring documentation is a mean strategy of white sovereignty that discredits "interior knowledge" of racialized people.[1] Rich's effort to cognitively understand whiteness and racial difference instead of affectively aligning herself with Lorde and trying to "bear witness" (as in acknowledge, remember, and indicate that the testimony has been of consequence) is an important illustration of how meanness operates as a type of civility that gatekeeps feminist sense-making.[2]

Justification through documentation is the white institutional vernacular that girlbosses have taken up as enabling feminist embourgeoisement. I open with this conflict between Lorde and Rich because the dialogue captures how feminism is often built on a politics of identity recognition, where only some parts of identity are purportedly valued, while other parts of identity requires reasoning for their existence and acceptance. Put another way, there is a "division between the women who write and speak feminism and the women who live it, the women who have voice versus the women who have experience, the ones who make the theories and policies and the ones who bear scars and sutures from the fight."[3] In this instance, Rich recognizes Lorde's identity, but demands documentation for her racial marginalization. The exchange between Lorde and Rich encapsulates how feminist affect is extended to subjects who can intelligibly complain about power dynamics, but *not* to subjects who cannot discourse and articulate their lived experience to the conditions of power. Not able to articulate in accordance to Western standards, Lorde is abjectified, and her work is appropriated to support Rich's lesbian continuum.[4] As Alexander Weheliye explicates of the subaltern's interior knowledge and capacity to articulate, "minority discourses seemingly cannot inhabit the space of proper theoretical reflection. . . . What is at stake is not so much the lack of language per se, since we have known for a while now that the subaltern cannot speak, but the kinds of dialects available to the subjected and how these are seen and heard by those who bear witness to their plight."[5] Sara Ahmed places emphasis instead on the feminist ear: "While a snap might seem to make the tongue the organ of feminist rebellion, perhaps snap is all about ears."[6]

It is no surprise then that a feminism that recognizes subaltern inarticulateness only for a few also recognizes feminist politics and expression only for a few. This is what Lauren Berlant calls the juxtapolitical: "It can be open toward politics but is abundantly on the outside of it, refusing its status as determining the real of power, agency, or experience."[7] Postfeminism's actors and texts are often accused of lacking politics, and of featuring instead aimless feminine expression as well as disarticulateness between language and power. Postfeminism is the pejorative name for discourses that assume that feminist struggle is over and done, that can attack feminism and celebrate cis-heteropatriarchy, even while nodding toward the importance of gender analysis. But, what if postfeminism is a site that allows feminism to disavow white fragility and encourage gender-only analysis? In my view, the construction of postfeminism makes explicit and justifies the marginalization of the subaltern within feminism. Feminism's critique of postfeminism is a confession of its exclusionary politics—its ableism, its anti-queer and transphobic sentiment, and its colonial and capitalist interests. Subaltern people may desire not being discriminated against, not harmed, not oppressed, but they may not be able to articulate that in equity, diversity, and inclusion lingo that has become co-opted by institutions. The subaltern may not have the feminist vernacular, but that should not make them less feminist. This mean girl feminism relies on the sex binary in order to gatekeep who is and who is not feminist: the feminist must be able to speak articulately about the sex binary and women's oppression.

The postfeminist is depicted as expressing ideas that make little sense and that deny power relations. Beauty, especially the hyperfeminine body, has become a common signifier of postfeminism and a marker of male gaze interest. In its critique of power relations, feminism suspects the postfeminist body for preventing self- and collective realization of its goals. Feminist scholars have called this postfeminist phenomenon, in which success appears to come with beauty in patriarchy, the *beauty myth*.[8] Two books in particular stand out for their popularity and prestige both inside and outside the field of gender studies: Susan Douglas's *Enlightened Sexism: The Seductive Message That Feminism's Work Is Done* (2010), and its main source of inspiration, Angela McRobbie's *The Aftermath of Feminism: Gender, Culture, and Social Change* (2009). At the center of their critique is McRobbie's concept of illegible rage.[9] Because modern womanhood does not celebrate gender fluidity and withholds social critique, girls and women in the postfeminist era must disguise their bid for leadership and other forms of betterment through beauty, fashion, and heteronormative sexuality, which McRobbie calls the feminine masquerade. McRobbie explains that the feminine masquerade regulates feminist rage by rendering such rage unintelligible and making fashion and beauty the culturally appropriate outlets to vent that rage.[10]

This line of feminist critique by McRobbie and Douglas illustrates how postfeminism becomes a point of contention rather than the condition of possibility for white feminist engagement. As a signifier that only white women allow to appear, feminism creates labels like postfeminism and neoliberal feminism (or any name other than white feminism) and displaces its shortcomings onto those labels. This strategy of considering the continued harms of patriarchy and capitalism through other labels is a trap of racial digression and diversion that allows feminism to preserve itself as postfeminism's more ethical s/cister and continually avoids intersectional accountability. In this chapter, I explore the ways in which feminism has understood difference and its own aberrations as postfeminist, and I trace how that difference of postfeminism figures into, resists, and alters the realization of feminism. To make sense of the relationship between feminism and postfeminism, I apply Jacques Derrida's concept-metaphor of the supplement, which is not just a mere add-on: "The supplement supplements. It adds only to replace. It intervenes or insinuates itself in-the-place-of; if it fills, it is as if one fills a void."[11] I argue that postfeminism has supplemented white feminism in the Derridean sense of the term: postfeminism is not a mere add-on to good liberal feminism but has replaced it, rendering feminism unintelligible to itself.

I also turn to McRobbie and Douglas's concept of illegible rage in order to reframe it as white feminist fragility. McRobbie and Douglas's concept of illegible rage infuses feminism with meanness toward inarticulate beauty and postfeminism, instead of toward the power relations of imperialist white supremacist capitalist cis-heteropatriarchy. Not a political misdirection of postfeminism, illegible rage should be seen as both a feminist problem and a racialized barrier to engaging with sovereign power. Derrida explicates the danger that the supplement poses: "The supplement is maddening because it is neither presence nor absence and because it consequently breaches both our pleasure and our virginity."[12] Following the logic of the supplement, postfeminism defies the language of metaphysics: it is present because feminism has not yet arrived or already has, and, at the same time, it is absent because feminism must stay at the horizon and in the realm of the possible. Postfeminist texts generate pleasure as a simple, pure expression of gender empowerment, a pleasure that feminism opens up but simultaneously forecloses. In other words, postfeminism encourages gender consciousness as a form of empowerment that can bring about pleasure. But, to give a feeling of resistance, feminism participates in a politics of antipleasure that deploys meanness and requires rage.

I begin with an analysis of the mean girl trope in the movie *Mean Girls* (2004), where the mean girl's beauty and popularity inhibit the intelligibility of the nice girl protagonist. Entitled to the male gaze too, the nice girl undergoes a makeover, shops, and strategizes to expose the mean girl's meanness and validate her own rightful place and innocence under the male gaze. From there, I examine the concept of illegible rage in *The Aftermath of Feminism* and *Enlightened Sexism*, which also plays out the mean girl trope in order to demonstrate postfeminism as an aberration of feminist goals. McRobbie and Douglas condemn the heteronormative male gaze for underwriting postfeminist interest in social approval and curtailing the popularity of feminism, rendering feminism and feminist scholarship innocent in the process. I show how both postfeminist fiction/media and feminist theory aim for a similar resolution: to locate productive outlets for releasing white feminine rage by reorienting women and girls to feminist principles that source oppression based on being a woman/girl. I argue that feminism strategically misrecognizes postfeminism as other—antifeminist, violent, mean—rather than as its own counterpart. This misrecognition allows feminism to project itself as nonviolent and progressive, ridding the world of meanness. To pursue such obfuscation, feminism constructs a binary of white mean postfeminists (who make feminism impossible) and white nice feminists (who cannot articulate a feminist politic for which postfeminists are to blame). Through the mean girl trope and the feminist/postfeminist divide, feminism denies its own inarticulateness and weaponizes an articulateness that it never had.

Mean Girl Trope

In gatekeeping appropriate feminine performativity, mean girl feminism singles out meanness only to disavow its own use of the strategy. Whereas Bitch feminism focuses on performativity with a feminist purpose, mean girl feminism explores its obverse: its goal is to expose meanness and competition for the male gaze as antifeminist performativity. As a lesson in feminist civility and the politics of antipleasure and negation, the exposure of meanness validates white feminine interiority and virtue by pointing to gender-based oppression as the central determinant of the subjectivity of white women. Calling out meanness imparts the idea that mean girls' dominance under the male gaze undermines nice girls' intelligibility and forestalls attempts to articulate feminist solidarity. The mean girl trope demonstrates how the feminist/postfeminist divide helps feminism evade its own lack of articulation and power analysis, obscuring an understanding of its demands; the strategies, tactics, and forms of communicative labor used to achieve them; and the ways performativity alone does not accomplish a feminist refusal of the male gaze but is a structural and interlocking relation to white sovereign power.

According to Elizabeth Behm-Morawitz and Dana Mastro's study of the top-grossing teen films of 1995–2005, "the longstanding picture of the 'cloyingly sweet and kind' girl presented in the media has been replaced by a new dominant image, that of the 'mean girl.'"[13] Contributing to that dominant image, the movie *Mean Girls* (2004) was considered a groundbreaking movie because it was written by a woman and self-proclaimed feminist, Tina Fey, and depicted the negative effects of high school cliques on girls (inspired by Rosalind Wiseman's 2002 parenting self-help book *Queen Bees and Wannabees*).[14] Even though the mean girl trope preexisted it (e.g., *Heathers* [1998]), *Mean Girls* marked the beginning of a film genre within women's popular culture (e.g., *You Again* [2010], *I Feel Pretty* [2018], and *Bridesmaids* [2011]) and has become a popular culture phenomenon itself, inspiring memes, memorable quotes, themed events and products, and spin-offs including a video game and stage musical. The cinematic narrative follows a white American girl named Cady Heron (Lindsay Lohan), previously homeschooled in Africa, and her entry into an American high school. Two school outsiders—Janis Ian (Lizzy Caplan), a racially ambiguous girl, and Damian Leigh (Daniel Franzese), a gay white boy—become her friends and help her assess who's who, with a cafeteria map of cliques, including the popular, white, wealthy girl squad known as the Plastics. After learning that Cady has been invited to eat lunch with the Plastics, Janis urges Cady to first inform her of their activities and later sabotage Regina George (Rachel McAdams), the "queen bee" of the Plastics. While undermining Regina's friendships with Gretchen Wieners (Lacey Chabert) and Karen Smith (Amanda Seyfried), tricking Regina into gaining weight, and exposing Regina's affair to her boyfriend, Cady is introduced to the "burn book" where the Plastics collect mean comments about other students. When Cady undergoes a makeover by adopting a new wardrobe and postfeminist vernacular, becoming queen bee herself, an estranged Regina makes copies of the burn book for the whole school. Principal Ron Duvall (Tim Meadows) calls an assembly in which Ms. Norbury (played by Fey) leads female students in expressing their rage through confessions of their mean "girl-on-girl" crime, then apologizing and performing trust falls.

While Regina is positioned as the queen bee, with Gretchen and Karen her wannabee friends who "work" for her by distributing mean affects, it becomes clear by the end of the movie that Cady was just as mean as Regina, as Janis points out to her and Cady eventually realizes. In *Enlightened Sexism*, Susan Douglas explains that the movie illustrates the problem of an unforgiving standard of womanhood and the role girls play in policing one another.[15] However, Douglas does not consider the question of how feminist meanness animates and reinforces racialized power dynamics, and neglects to interrogate the efficacy of dividing feminism and postfeminism. How Cady is actively misrecognized as a nice, well-intentioned girl even as she employs the logic of meanness is crucial to the bifurcation of feminism and postfeminism.

At this level, *Mean Girls* suggests that womanhood reciprocating the male gaze is the main obstacle to feminism's realization. The conflict between Cady and Regina is spurred by Janis, who, though her actual sexual orientation is never revealed, falls victim to Regina's homophobia. When Cady becomes queen bee and chooses not to invite Janis and Damian to her party, Janis confronts Cady: "Hey, buddy, you're not pretending anymore. You're plastic. Cold, shiny, hard plastic." But, Janis is not positioned as a mean girl: she is a social outsider, and her marginality in the school prevents her from occupying the queen bee status and from reinforcing white feminist civility. Instead, Regina is seen as the ultimate mean girl: she embodies the feminist problem of repressed rage, which at the end of the movie is channeled into contact sports, and the scene in which she is hit by a bus provides cathartic and karmic relief for her meanness. Cady's on-task fascination in verifying Regina's meanness and her own background as an outsider who was homeschooled in Africa for most of her life positions Cady as an innocent white girl caught up in unfortunate circumstances. Ensnared in the web of exposing meanness, Cady is invested in obtaining social approval that can corroborate her perception of Regina and validate her own moral virtue. Cady's middle-classness further buttresses her ordinariness and innocence, for she is perceived as operating outside of Regina's practices of embourgeoisement to be(come) queen bee. The violence Cady caused is forgiven in the end because Cady seeks redemption through her friendships with Janis and Damian. The movie's conclusion suggests that the violence from both white girls was misguided and inconsistent with their inherent virtue. The (post)feminist solution of redirecting white women's rage to nonviolent outlets is an example of how coalition building can sidestep difficult, possibly inarticulate, conversations about power.[16] Nevertheless, Regina and Cady share much in common, and both of their trajectories (and the problems that they face) appear rooted in the category of gender rather than racialized as white fragility.

At another level, civility in *Mean Girls* is structured by feminist disavowal of white embodiment. On Cady's first day sitting with the Plastics, Gretchen declares that there are strict instructions about appropriate dress, hair, and etiquette that dictate their "Girl World" and are "the rules of feminism." If Girl World is depicted as a peculiar postfeminist space that seizes feminism, then the "Animal World" appropriates stereotypes about Africa and alludes to Black hostility. Cady compares the physical fighting of animals "in heat" in the Animal World to the "sneaky" passive-aggressive fighting of the Girl World, a framing that provokes her own strategies of sabotage. Cady's previous experiences in Africa are used to deny her white racial embodiment and to conceptualize and imagine her as other. From the way that she is expected to be Black on the first day of class, to Cady being asked why she is white if she is from Africa, to her nickname "Africa," Cady's past operates as an immaterial otherness. By labeling the other Black students as "unfriendly Black hotties"—and showing Cady's childhood love to be a Black boy who runs away from her—*Mean Girls* deploys Blackness as a visible point of contrast to Cady's white feminine virtue. When Cady becomes queen bee, the two worlds collapse, devolving into "full-tilt jungle madness." Thus, Blackness and racialization function as the background through which feminist civility can be depicted and reimagined as better than the postfeminist Girl World and racialized Animal World. With the eventual acceptance of Cady in a multicultural liberal feminist setting, anxiety about white feminine performativity in securing embourgeoisement remains disarticulated and is deferred until new mean girls enter the scene.

My analysis of *Mean Girls* shows how feminism deploys the mean girl figure to excuse its own violent participation in meanness. The deferral of feminism due to the postfeminist mean girl figure illustrates how "the modern subject often employs its reflexive capacities not to transform its own relation to the iconic sign but to build up a fantasy of a corrupted other that prevents the sign from operating in the proper way and delivering on its redemptive promises."[17] The figuration of the mean girl is that "corrupted other." Through the mean girl trope, feminism simultaneously projects gender-based marginalization on white misbehavior and transgressions and redirects that rage onto culturally appropriate outlets within imperial white supremacist capitalist patriarchy. Mean girl feminism considers white girls and women as the victims and perpetrators of meanness and allows white girls, after recognizing the importance of feminism and the category of gender, to seek redemption for their violence. Feminism defers an engagement with the violence of white women's performativity by blaming meanness for feminism's nonarrival.

While this movie was lauded as helping initiate a feminist conversation about postfeminist meanness among girls and women, I want to compare it to a precursor, *Clueless* (1995) (which we might be more tempted to dismiss as simply postfeminist), because *Clueless* provides important insight into the relationship between white womanhood and (post)feminism. Featuring a vapid, hyperfeminine girl living in Beverly Hills, Cher Horowitz (Alicia Silverstone), *Clueless* may not count as a feminist text because Cher's cluelessness does not offer an admirable model of gender performativity. *Clueless* has many motifs of the mean girl trope, as queen bee Cher and her best friend, Dionne Davenport (Stacey Dash), give the new girl, Tai Frasier (Brittany Murphy), a makeover, and Tai eventually becomes queen bee herself. Cher's queen bee status stems from her attainment of white bourgeois beauty standards, and likewise, her meanness toward others (like yelling "as if" to the guy who puts his arm around her) is related to maintaining those girlboss standards. Meanness in *Clueless* follows the beauty myth logic that girls' and women's success can be owed to the male gaze. From Miss Geist's (Twink Caplan) harsh grading practices to Tai's insults as queen bee, Cher resolves their meanness by redirecting their affective energy to white male desire and affirmation. Nevertheless, Cher's liberal humanitarianism and willingness to do good are what make her a likable character and manage the discursive violence of white feminine virtue. Her decision to "make over her soul," including spearheading Pismo Beach disaster relief efforts, compensates for her cluelessness and inarticulateness. Whereas *Mean Girls* makes gender-based marginalization the explicit foundation for postfeminist meanness, *Clueless* shows how postfeminist meanness arises from cluelessness, inarticulateness, and lack of maturity stemming from gender norms and expectations. But, both movies suggest that white feminine virtue can be revived and redeemed through gendered acknowledgment of power, even if not fully articulate or even if broken up by hedges and "like" language.[18] Thus, if anything, the postfeminism of *Clueless* is indicative of the egoism within feminist scholarship and the feminist refusal to acknowledge the pleasure in white feminine performativity that may come with single-gender analysis. In other words, postfeminist accusations allow feminism to be fascinated by the white hyperfeminine body and, at the same time, to put forward an antipleasure with performativity that is at the center of feminism's own politics and possibility.

Mean Girls of Feminist Scholarship

Having demonstrated how mean girl feminism constructs civility in popular culture through the trope of mean girls, I want now to interrogate how feminist scholarship theorizes meanness as a postfeminist competitive mode of resistance that prevents feminist articulation and realization. I read this postfeminist or neoliberal feminist turn as symptomatic of white supremacy, as Ruby Hamad eloquently writes: "We cannot even conceive of let alone manifest a world without white supremacy if we don't see it for what it is: a persistent group delusion that externalizes all of the characteristics of itself that it doesn't like—and from which feminism is not exempt."[19] Feminist scholarship has situated (post)feminism as a conflicted set of discourses aimed at creating backlash against women's rights. One line of feminist inquiry focuses on the production of female hostility as an effect of the male gaze. This line of inquiry demonstrates how "feminism has been a much better resource for critique than for providing accounts of how to live amid affective uncertainty, ambivalence, and incoherence."[20]

Susan Douglas's *Enlightened Sexism* argues that the media from the 1990s on has represented feminism as having accomplished its goals, culminating in a rash of postfeminist girls and women who no longer know their place and are too empowered. In response to this "perceived threat of a new gender regime," Douglas writes, the media has adopted a framework of "enlightened sexism": recirculating sexist images and stereotypes and presenting these as aspirational for young women.[21] Examples of postfeminism from popular culture abound: from the catty women of the *Real Housewives* (2006–) franchise, to the young women of *Girls Gone Wild* (1997–2011), who perform their "agency" through/to flashing cameras.[22] Douglas's chapters are organized around representations of womanhood that repudiate feminism. In a chapter titled "Lean and Mean," Douglas discusses the obsession with beauty as the source of competition among women. She elaborates on the mean girl phenomenon: "The bitch—assertive, snotty, self-important and self-absorbed, confrontational, outspoken, hypercritical, a threat to men and a danger to other women, and, typically, rich—has become one of the required stock characters in reality TV."[23] From the popular girl to the bitch, every female character type is set up to be repellent and doomed to illegible rage. Inspired by Angela McRobbie's notion of illegible rage, Douglas contends that because women are barred from identifying with and directing their rage toward the patriarchy, women direct meanness at other women. Douglas concludes her book by advocating for the importance of governmental reform but says that two obstacles stand in the way: the media's poor depiction of women, and the need to reclaim the term *feminism* for political action.

Douglas's advocacy for a legislatively driven feminism insinuates that postfeminism fails to be oriented around political action and can be blamed for patriarchy's continued success. However, I view this line of argumentation as problematic for two reasons. First, it treats politics as a separate arena of life rather than a quotidian part of living, or what Ronald Walter Greene might call "a politics of living labor."[24] Her feminism separates subjects who have the time and resources to commit to political advocacy from subjects who "live labor" and may not be canvasing or campaigning for Capital Hill but who have lives that are no less affected by politics. This bifurcation has the additional effect of unmooring feminism from the lived experience of the working class and racialized peoples, as Rafia Zakaria poignantly notes: not only are "[the so-called] real feminists . . . fighting for the cause in the public arena untrammeled by the shifting burden of messy experience," but also "the stories of women of color are often told but the perspective gained from living such stories never becomes part of the epistemology of feminism."[25]

The second problematic element of Douglas's feminism is that it is motivated by an anxiety around white feminist embourgeoisement and the way that whiteness and white performativity do not necessarily signify feminism. If the performative turn in Bitch feminism suggests that a political commitment to feminism can be read on the body, then the white feminine body and certain aspects of speech and bodily comportment, like dress and makeup, are no longer stable referents of feminist identity in mean girl feminism . The problem with postfeminist politics is not only that the postfeminist woman has none, but also that her performativity is not seen as a signifier of protesting patriarchy. The concern over feminism becoming depoliticized is rooted in the instability of white womanhood as the "conduit" of resistance to cis-heteropatriarchy.[26] The performative turn that links the body to bitchiness and meanness tries to restabilize white womanhood and reposition white feminine performativity as that from which protest and emancipation are supposed to emanate.

To end with further worry about the state of feminism, Douglas considers if and how patriarchal change is possible. She asks with disbelief: "Who would have believed we could elect an African American man president of the United States?"[27] By posing this question, Douglas unwittingly suggests that Black futurity is closer in reach than feminist futurity is, and she traffics in the historical tensions that marked suffragette feminism, when white women's advancement was predicated on the continued oppression of people of color.[28] At the same time, Douglas uses Black achievement to analogically think through feminist futurity by implying that Barack Obama's presidential win is indicative of an institutional capacity for minoritized inclusion. Douglas's notion of feminist futurity envisions the need to recommit to the category of gender by minimizing through comparison, to borrow from Lorde, the "empowering joy" of solidarity in Obama's win.[29] Carrying on white feminism's legacy, Douglas reiterates Blackness as an abject omen of feminism's failure and deferral.

Much of Douglas's feminist analysis and inspiration are drawn from Angela McRobbie's *The Aftermath of Feminism*, a sophisticated sociological study on how feminism operates as a neoliberal form of advancement. For McRobbie, feminism has become a Gramscian common sense, through which subjects and institutions are encouraged to be gender aware or to have already "taken [gender] into account."[30] With global capitalism's increased reliance on women and girls for labor, positive messaging about feminist leadership situates girls and women as economic subjects whose potential can be realized by participating in flexible global capitalism. Thus, unhinging feminism from critiques of power has allowed feminine performativity to become susceptible to neoliberal appropriation. Although McRobbie acknowledges that the neoliberal rhetoric of confidence and empowerment that overlays with feminist discourse makes it difficult to address other discriminatory practices and institutions, her analysis of the disarticulation of feminism demonstrates a melancholic attachment to the politics of white feminine performativity rather than a willingness to reformulate notions of feminist liberation and freedom.

To theorize the concept of illegible rage as misdirected affect resulting from the feminine masquerade, McRobbie's analysis reinscribes the mean girl trope into feminism by assuming that feminine performativity needs to be oriented toward a politics that McRobbie too does not articulate. One way she reinscribes the mean girl trope is by moralizing participation in the male gaze on the part of two polar-opposite characters who are enamored with men: Bridget Jones (Renée Zellweger) from *Bridget Jones's Diary* (2001), who wants nothing more than to fall in love and get married, and Alex Forrest (Glenn Close) from *Fatal Attraction* (1987), who refuses the social contract on extramarital affairs. McRobbie's critique centers on how the goals of postfeminist women are oriented around men and pleasure rather than politics and power. Another way she reinscribes the mean girl trope is that she discusses her international students as subjects who participate in flexible capitalism and, therefore, do not threaten the West because they do not challenge the intimate connections between flexible capitalism and Western global hegemony. Her critique is perplexing given that international student attraction to learn academically in the West is in part made possible by the academy's creation of the category of gender, which then solicits people from the Global South to leave their colonized homelands in the first place. In other words, her critique creates a trap that bifurcates the academy: the teachers are feminist, and the students are misguided and postfeminist. While illegible rage is a valuable concept, her application of it fails to grasp the relationship between the feminine masquerade, whiteness, and global capital. Indeed, I want to ask: To whom is the rage illegible? Whose rage is illegible? What if illegible rage is a strategy of whiteness? What if illegible rage theorizes, instead, white women who believe that gender oppression is a legitimate reason to be mean to everyone, especially racialized, queer, trans, disabled peoples, and anyone else left out of their category of woman?

Illegible rage is fundamental to white colonial feminism and its authoritative hold on criticizing cis-heteropatriarchy. If illegible rage comes into being by confronting cis-heteropatriarchy, I propose two examples of mean girls' illegible rage that demonstrate the concept's intersectional potential in theorizing the subaltern's inarticulateness: Jean Cabot (Sandra Bullock) in the award-winning movie *Crash* (2004), and the main characters of the television show *Desperate Housewives* (2004–12). In *Crash*, a movie about interracial encounters and their ensuing racial conflict, Jean is a white woman who appears to be mean to everyone and rationalizes her rage as justified. She accuses her husband, district attorney Rick (Brendan Fraser), of being patronizing after a carjacking incident. She suspects the locksmith Daniel Ruiz (Michael Peña) of being a "gang member," and says that she knew she would be subject to violence when walking by two Black men. After getting upset with her housekeeper, Maria (Yomi Perry), too, Jean calls a friend to complain about how she is angry at everyone and everything: "I just thought that I would wake up today and I would feel better. You know, but I was still mad and I realized that it had nothing to do with my car being stolen. I wake up like this every morning. I am angry all the time and I don't know why." With that revelation, she falls down the stairs, a metaphor for toppling from her pedestal. After Maria takes her to the hospital, Jean telephones Rick to say how her best friends would not respond to her emergency and then hugs Maria, confessing to her that she is "the best friend I've got." These scenes encourage viewers to notice illegible rage and question a white feminist common sense that has gone awry: What are Jean's struggles? What makes Jean's life hard? How is Jean oppressed? Jean's misguided rage is a result of white supremacy's deployment of feminism: how the category of gender stunts her recognition of her own privilege, rendering her an unlikable character who needs to be taken down by way of an accidental fall, much like Regina. Jean's illegible rage is an inarticulate affect of single-issue gender analysis, misdirected at everyone, regardless of their racialized positionality as white men and as employees of color. In dramatizing a confrontation with cis-heteropatriarchy, mean girl feminism imagines privileged white women against the world because their work-life balance is too much to handle, their quotidian routine is too stressful, their family is too demanding, and, in general, all basic needs and aspects of their lives are not privileges, but burdens to the very being of white womanhood. In this way, illegible rage is nothing more than the rage of an unsatisfied master of white feminism.

Another example of illegible rage can be seen in the characters of *Desperate Housewives*, a television series set on seemingly perfect suburban Wisteria Lane with less than perfect women and their families, who come together after their friend and neighbor Mary Alice Young (Brenda Strong) dies by suicide. The title of the show evokes Betty Friedan's "problem that has no name" for white privileged housewives, whose unhappiness is derived from their unrealized potential and lack of domestic fulfillment.[31] The characters' efforts to keep work and family life happy and orderly are similar to Jean's, in that they appear to emerge from the category of gender rather than race, and the housewives' book club on *Madame Bovary* encourages audiences to read the show against patriarchy. With illegible rage that stems from envy and from idealized expectations about gender and domestic responsibilities, the housewives experience, variously, obsessive-compulsive levels of perfection (Bree Van de Kamp [Marcia Cross]), competition for a love interest (Susan Mayer [Teri Hatcher]), unappeasable desire for male attention (Gabrielle

Solis [Eva Longoria]), and an overwhelming sense of domestic incompetence (Lynette Scavo [Felicity Huffman]). The single-gender context implies that each of these problems is an obstacle created by patriarchy that prevents a progressive performance of womanhood. While the feminist show assumes patriarchy as its background and counterpoint, what the characters—both white and non-white—can and cannot do is made possible by whiteness. By acknowledging patriarchy and gender constructs without naming and articulating their problems, *Desperate Housewives* depicts mean girl performativity as a white feminist response to the housewives' unhappiness. Lynette's commitment to family order (and consequent failure to meet it) justifies her illegible rage toward everyone—from a police officer, to her partner, to other parents, and eventually to her own children.[32] Because envy operates as "pure culture of the death drive—a spoiling hatred which is directed at one and the same time against the admired (for its fantasized cohesion and power) and the despised (because it contains the projected rejects of the self)," Lynette repeats her illegible rage at those she admires and those she despises, especially men.[33] When Lynette is stopped by a white male police officer because her children are not buckled properly into their seats, his suggestion that it is her "job" to ensure their safety prompts Lynette to lose her temper. Contrary to how *Desperate Housewives* narrates Lynette's misdirected rage and desperation as feminist in nature—the voice-over attributes her outburst to the fact that she is a woman being told how to raise her children—I want to suggest that her illegible rage is rooted in the insecure status of white feminism and feminist performativity as a master logic and signifier. As with a Karen who is caught on camera yelling at low-wage workers and people of color, Lynette's illegible rage arises from her realization that her own white feminine body and performativity are not special, and she must abide by the rule of law. The illegible rage of white women should raise the very question of white feminism's capacity to be a better master (signifier).

In feminist meanness, performativity slides into simple embodiment and nonperformativity. The connection between patriarchal revolt and white feminine performativity appears intuitive and unnamed because, as Friedan's book too failed to consider, the housewives' situation of being unhappy—with the privilege of having the "occupation" of a housewife, and the ability to depend on merely their husband's job and wealth—is tied to whiteness. When a former work colleague tells Lynette that she was like a "shark" (and therefore a valuable worker and likely leader), her "yearning" to be seen as more than childcare giver and family food preparer emanates from how white supremacy reveres white women's labor above that of people of color.

Amid their discussions of the failures of feminism, it is hard not to conclude that McRobbie and Douglas (and many self-proclaimed feminist theorists and critics) have a deep longing for feminism to mean something more than girl empowerment amid global capitalism's production of the beauty myth, fashion-beauty complex, and values of neoliberal self-improvement. Their concern about feminism's disarticulation from patriarchal power arises from the threat that postfeminism's overexposure, saturation, and normalization of white feminine performativity pose to feminism. That is, postfeminism marks the idea that feminism is nothing more than a sign, an idol that "provides ideological cover, socially acceptable ways of relating to power."[34] My two examples of illegible rage, from *Crash* and *Desperate Housewives*, show how white women and white womanhood embody white sovereignty and power in ways that are disavowed by single-issue gender analysis. Moreover, McRobbie and Douglas's notion of illegible rage falls short because their examples are analyzed for the antagonistic relationship between men and women or patriarchy and feminism rather than for the way that subalternity is produced through (post)feminist expression. What has been labeled postfeminism is feminism's afterlife of naturalizing white women who can love cis-heteropatriarchy, love within it, and love to complain about their attachment to it.

Conclusion

This chapter illustrates how popular feminism and feminist scholarship have broadly appropriated Blackness and racialization for the sole purpose of revealing that gender oppression continues. Significantly, feminism's misrecognition of postfeminism promotes gender consciousness as a key characteristic of the feminist archive and of what counts as feminist. In its singular focus on gender, feminism stresses how womanhood requires constant maintenance to meet unrealistic standards around beauty, relationality, and occupational worth to thrive in patriarchy, all the while advocating for including the voice(s) of white women as a marker of equity and justice. To patiently care for children while in heels, to work while wearing makeup that smears, to cook and clean for oneself (and others) to a bourgeois standard of living: much of what can be interpreted as staying afloat and trying to make it as a woman also intersects with a feeling of keeping up with appearances and participating in embourgeoisement. As demonstrated in my analyses of the movie *Mean Girls* and feminist scholarship on illegible rage, the mean girl trope operates as an important mechanism through which feminism can construct appropriate gender performativity in an era marked by postfeminist competition and disarticulation. Shaming the mean girl and locating evidence of her meanness avoids articulating a feminist politic, reinforcing the very problem of stalled feminist solidarity that meanness caused in the first place. Feminist disarticulation from power relations as well as an ambiguity of feminist goals help establish feminist performativity and civility as an amorphous site for gender analysis and criticism, a site that is unbounded by race. This rhetorical strategy of structural misrecognition of feminism and postfeminism promotes melancholic clinging to mean performativity and a reinvention of the category of gender instead of a reimagining of feminism as a form of human emancipation and liberation.

The illegible rage of white womanhood is the meanness of unrealized and struggling white masters and girlbosses; Cady is mean until the liberal feminist realizes that she is the girlboss, Regina is mean and even more enraged when she loses queen bee status, Jean's meanness is an effect of being a vulnerable woman, and Lynette could have been a girlboss. Blackness operates as a counterpoint and background through which feminism can scapegoat mean girls and women for adhering to postfeminism and not pledging allegiance to feminism. Feminist meanness is an illegible rage that has no particular targets, and—as Lorde made clear to Rich in the conversation that opened this chapter—suppresses "perception" and "interior knowledge" that are necessary for solidarity with the subaltern. Feminist scholarship does not gesture toward the unfinished idea of what justice and equality are but rather rants, rages, and justifies itself against postfeminism's aimlessness and inarticulateness. By misrecognizing postfeminism as other than itself, feminism allows itself "to reappear as the source of solutions to our problems with it, as the ideal answer to the dismal anxiety it provokes."[35]

As this chapter has shown, by channeling meanness toward postfeminism, feminism can ignore its own racial implications and relationship to colonial violence. The next chapter looks outward from the mean girl herself to her interpersonal relationships, discussing power couple feminism as a form of civility that domesticates white aggression, transmuting it into a heteronormative love matrix of power and affection. The chapter shows how *power couple* emerges as a term to circumscribe women in modern heteronormative relationships, including ones involving aggression. Power couple feminism ultimately rehabilitates violent white men as lovable through their partnership with mean white women, who in turn are redeemed as their saviors.

CHAPTER 3

POWER COUPLE FEMINISM

Gaslighting and Re-Empowering
Heteronormative Aggression

In a sketch titled "Biracial Dating Is Complicated" from the comedy television show *Key & Peele* (2012–15), Keegan-Michael Key plays Jeff, a biracial man on a date with a white woman, who asks him to bounce between white Jeff and Black Jeff in his interactions with the restaurant staff. She explains that she "read somewhere that when you date a biracial guy you get the best of both worlds." She mouths "Black Jeff" or winks or side-eyes to prompt him to act aggressive and protective as Black Jeff, or to be polite and deferential as white Jeff. I start with this skit not only to demonstrate the acute deftness expected of racialized people (who must code-switch and navigate imperialist white supremacist capitalist cis-heteropatriarchy even while being objectified by it) but also to show how white womanhood attempts to mobilize Jeff as part of a power couple—an extension of herself, for her defense, for her goals. This sketch illustrates the power couple feminist logic in which white women judge a man's potential as a partner based on his capacity to marshal his resources (in this case, his race) for her purpose, which also becomes their purpose.

In 2016, the *Oxford English Dictionary* updated its list of entries to include *power couple*. According to the *Huffington Post*, this change was newsworthy because the term was the "new standard of relationship success": it is a two-word, compound entry that describes how both partners, often heterosexual, are "successful in their own right."[1] The concept long preceded the term, dating back to Antony and Cleopatra, and includes such notable pairings as Sonny and Cher, Bill and Melinda Gates, Brad Pitt and Angelina Jolie, and Ivanka Trump and Jared Kushner. Neither partner need be a self-proclaimed feminist, but the term evokes the male partner's respect for the woman's career by sharing household and childcare responsibilities or by being her biggest fan. While the term suggests that the woman's professional actualization is the cause for domestic equality, respect, and nonhierarchical love, the term deemphasizes the fact that the man's contribution may be merely passive permission for her to pursue professional success. Furthermore, the term conjures a neoliberal form of mathematics where individual agency is enhanced when one is allied with another person's career, resources, and capital: more can be achieved when together than when alone. The term *power couple* marks how feminism propelled women into the workplace in such a way as to benefit rather than hurt heterosexual marital arrangements, position women as independent and ambitious self-governing individuals, and undergird the importance of equity for modern relationships. The term *power couple* proposes a model of heterosexual relationship that is workable for feminist goals by refiguring white women's attachment to cis-heteropatriarchy and white men. However, are power couples a new form of feminism?

With special attention to creating monogamous romance, power couples reanimate "the insular 'my family first' ethos" that white women use to ignore the politics of race and multicultural communities.[2] Moreover, power couple feminism appropriates the strategies and feelings of working in community and puts them toward the woman's own coupledom and family. If the power couple had a theme or entrance song, it might be Starship's "Nothing's Gonna Stop Us Now" (1987): "Let the world around us / Just fall apart . . . And we can build this dream together / Standing strong forever / Nothing's gonna stop us now." What matters in power couple feminism is not the world that is being created with ethical values but the monogamous love that shows women's "survival skills" in cis-heteropatriarchy: "getting men to fall in love with us, a form of self-protection that is also a female version of men's sexual conquering."[3] Importantly, although power couples can certainly have open relationships (as can be seen in this chapter), power couple feminism emphasizes how women can be empowered in monogamous relations and heteronormativity can become progressive support for feminism.

While *power couple* is popularly applied to celebrity pairings, its meaning extends beyond this usage, to encompass an idealization of romantic relationships with women who are independent and self-governed, especially mean girls. Similar to the mean girl, who finds her place within cis-heteropatriarchy by dominating attention, resources, and relations, power couples exemplify feminism's coexistence with cis-heteropatriarchy by offering an example of feminist happiness, love, and futurity in partnership with straight men. The term *power couple* provides marriage and coupledom with feminist purpose by combining love with work, the private sphere with the public, in ways that minimize the appearance of an unhealthy work-life balance. The term's use is indicative of what Sarah Banet-Weiser calls popular feminism, which celebrates heteronormativity, celebrity culture, and neoliberal forms of self-confidence and achievement.[4] The *work wife* is a play off of the *power couple* too, wherein women are encouraged to establish professional relationships with other women and to "eventually manipulate this partnership into increased mutual white-collar labor."[5] If the girl squad of work wives is a clique that takes the facade of feminist community building, then the power couple is a clique that reconciles feminist community building with heterosociality.

As discussed in the previous chapters, feminist theory and criticism have advanced the problem of meanness as a social affect of vying for or challenging the male gaze. For example, Sheryl Sandberg urges women to "lean in" and work toward helping one another, rather than competing like queen bees—a reference to a 1970s phenomenon in which a woman "in a leadership role, especially in male-dominated industries . . . used her position to keep other female 'worker bees' down."[6] Envy is imagined as the center of that hostility because patriarchal power supposes tokenistic limits on recognition (the male gaze can celebrate but one). While envy is usually seen as an "unjustified" and typically female response, the figure of the mean girl naturalizes envy by engaging in uncompromising comparison with others, including her object of affection, in order to be independent, confident, and ambitious.[7] In this chapter, envy operates differently than it does in previous chapters. Not just occurring among women, envy happens between men and women, a concern articulated by Wendy Brown when she writes that feminism may be "tethered to a formulation of justice that reinscribes a bourgeois (masculinist) ideal as its measure."[8]

To explore how the term and figuration of *power couple* mobilize white romantic relationships for feminism, I examine how heteronormative intimacy contains and structures white women's sovereignty as supporting white men, even when they are violent. Affection is not simply defined along a romantic or sexual plane; it circulates along social and financial planes as well. Thus, I read public expressions of love not simply as a feeling conveyed between two individuals, but as an affect that transforms the nature of the relationship itself. Also transformed are the visibility and agency of the two individuals, as well as the power matrix that offers their relationship intelligibility. Central to the heteronormative love matrix in neoliberalism, monogamous heteronormative relationality does more than simply economize the number of partners: it monopolizes the social and political energies of the individuals, fusing them into a neoliberal marital arrangement. I consider how the power couple operates as a white network of feminist affection in which love is most legible and visible when it contributes to embourgeoisement. Under the rubric of monogamous love, meanness enhances power couples' purchasing power, capacity to utilize social networks and resources, management of risk, and appeals to redistribute emotional labor. I argue that it is precisely because of the assumption of monogamous love that envy and jealousy are overlooked as structuring heteronormative relational aggression and the interpersonal dynamics that manage antagonism between feminism and cis-heteropatriarchy. With the singer Tina Turner, then, I ask: what's love got to do with it?[9]

By critically examining love and intimacy, I consider how power couple feminism reconciles the hostility of envy with the production of couple-dom or "group feeling." Following Sianne Ngai's theorization of envy as that which "lacks cultural recognition as a valid mode of publicly recognizing or responding to social disparities, even though it remains the *only* agonistic emotion defined as having a perceived inequality as its object," I analyze expressions of monogamous love as examples of envy of white male sovereignty.[10] The monogamous love from the mean girl produces sovereignty by suppressing antagonistic relations with outsiders and monopolizing the affective economy. To play on the Cartesian phrase of "I think, therefore I am," she may be mean, but she loves him, and therefore she is. In mean girl feminism, her feminist values and outlook make her virtuous and good; her meanness and wit make her sexy and attractive. In this way, the mean girl feminist is intelligible and compatible with patriarchy. I show that the queen bee's eventual monogamous affection and successful negotiation between intimate relations and work are used to render violent white men nonthreatening and lovable. My argument extends Ruby Hamad's words: "The concept of white women's virtue is a corollary of white men's sin: by keeping this false image of impeccable White Womanhood alive, white masculinity was absolved of its terrible crimes and Black sexuality could be demonized and mythologized."[11] I argue that power couple feminism and the attention to white feminist performativity by mean girls obscure how violent white men are rendered lovable by (mean) white women, who in turn are redeemed as their saviors.

I examine two key power couples in this chapter: one fictional, one not. The first is "queen bee" Blair Waldorf (Leighton Meester) and Chuck Bass (Ed Westwick) in *Gossip Girl* (2007–12), a television show about the lives and drama of upper-class teenagers in an elite, private high school (and university) on the Upper East Side of Manhattan, New York.[12] The second is 2016 presidential candidate Hillary Clinton and her husband, President Bill Clinton, whose case shows how white heteronormative intimacy can absolve violence that happens in other spaces. I choose these two examples to illustrate power couple feminism because, like in the skit with biracial Jeff, white feminist women mobilize their partners as if these men are feminist too. While their male partners have been accused of sexual violence and harassment, these feminist women gaslight by protecting, supporting, and continuing to love them.

In the former case, *Gossip Girl*'s namesake is a website where rumors and photos are submitted and made public. The show is a 121-episode story about a boy, Daniel Humphrey (Penn Badgley), who likes a girl, Serena van der Woodsen (Blake Lively): but instead of pulling her hair and teasing her on the playground, Dan creates a modern tool of harassment and surveillance, the Gossip Girl blog, which generates an audience of onlookers who treat Serena as the "it" girl by chronicling and judging her every move. At the same time, Dan uses the website to develop his own persona, Lonely Boy. While this perverse plot of courtship functions as the narrative arc of the show, this troubled scene of heterosexist love is deposed by the queen bee, Blair Waldorf. Her coming-of-age story interweaves her zealous efforts at embourgeoisement with the romantic rights and wrongs of being in the arms of bad boy Chuck Bass. Their love is a complementary balance of opposites, where Chuck's sexual predations and violent tendencies can find redemption only in the white mean girl's requited love. Similarly, the violent surveillance of Dan's Gossip Girl website is neutralized by Serena and Dan's nuptials. Throughout the show, the mean girl characters struggle to establish an equilibrium of adequate achievement and reputation that satisfies envy's reverent ebbs and aggressive flows between themselves and their significant others. When the mean girls have established their own "empire" and become sovereigns in their own right, their relationships appear ready for marriage.

Likewise, the power couple of Hillary and Bill is romanticized as a relationship that suppresses envy for love's fruition and for feminism's possibility and future in cis-heteropatriarchy. Through an analysis of the four-part documentary series *Hillary* (2020), which narrates Hillary's background and interest in politics, I argue that the romanticization of the Clintons' relationship as a political power couple displaces the violence of Bill's actions as external to Hillary's visibility and accomplishments. In other words, the power couple concept is seen as a pure expansion of feminist power in that Hillary is exposed for not standing up for feminist principles against white male violence.

If envy "can be used to explore the fraught issue of antagonism's political value for feminism, and to disclose the limitations of sympathetic identification as our culture's dominant way of understanding the making of female homosociality and the formation of political groups," then power couple feminism helps construct cis-heteropatriarchy as the realization of feminism's heteronormative sociality.[13] Power couple feminism smooths over the contradictions in work-life balance by establishing mean girls as sovereigns capable of love and salvation. In so doing, power couple feminism appears nonviolent and progressive, creating the possibility of redemption for white male harm.

The Mean Girl's Envy and Requited Love

Monogamy manages human sexuality and relationships in ways that are similar to the monopolies of neoliberal systems of corporate governance and autonomy, which dominate access to resources and goods while claiming to offer more worker benefits than harms. Like a monopoly, monogamy operates as a value that undergirds heteronormative judgment about the appropriateness of human interaction. Monogamy regulates practices of human sexuality by predetermining intentions in relationships, gatekeeping human interactions, and providing a rubric for what constitutes good romantic love. Cis-heteropatriarchy relies on monogamy to narrow women's goals to marriage, reduce women's companionship to heterosexual romance, and ensure the male role and significance in a reproductive future. According to Michel Foucault, heterosexual marriage shifted from a private concept that secured economic status to a system of shared duties or obligations that internally regulate and provide stability to the couple. Foucault argues that marriage helped establish and shape the art of governing oneself by demanding "a monopoly of pleasure" and offering an egalitarian reciprocity of fulfillment. He suggests that marriage supports rather than negates the feminist concern about work-life balance: "Marriage, as an individual tie capable of integrating relations of pleasure and of giving them a positive value, will constitute the most active focus for defining a stylistics of moral life."[14] Monogamy solidifies the sex binary that makes colonial sexualities appear more civilized by instituting and prioritizing white bourgeois values and morality.[15] As Sabine Broeck writes about white women's moral status alongside white men, "White Western women . . . had an entry into the social formation of the human, based on their share in the symbolic and material system of racist coloniality."[16] Heteronormative relationality gains feminist value in the concept of the white power couple.

Monogamy becomes the glamorous star of the show, with envy facilitating love's visibility and allure, on *Gossip Girl*. A running theme is how various outsiders of the social circle want to be like them, from the young girls sitting below the queen bee, to the character of Ivy (Kaylee DeFer), who tries to fit in by mimicking Serena. Even the ways that Blair and Serena fight as they vie for queen bee suggest that envy—the desire to take what the other has for themselves—is at the heart of their conflicts. The meanness that Serena and Blair distribute to those around them supports their embourgeoisement and manages the racial and class boundaries of their social circle. Dan's childhood friend Vanessa Abrams (Jessica Szohr), who is biracial, and Asian American peer Nelly Yuki (Yin Chang) are excluded from the all-white bourgeois clique, despite Nelly gaining the coveted admission to Yale University or Vanessa being offered the chance to deliver the freshman toast. When both Vanessa and Nelly get caught up in the meanness and envy themselves, they are written as minor characters of the show as meanness and envy do not reflect their character development.[17] Similarly, white middle-class Jenny (Taylor Momsen) fails to transgress class boundaries and is condemned to leave the Upper East Side.[18] Thus, white prestige in *Gossip Girl* determines who can use meanness, how, and to what effect. Furthermore, the feminization of meanness is maintained even when men act mean. For example, when Serena's brother Eric (Connor Paolo) humiliates Jenny, he is dumped by his partner, Jonathan (Matt Doyle), who accuses him of changing and becoming someone he is not. Like with other men on the show, Eric's meanness, aimed at teaching Jenny to stop her own meanness, is seen less as a feature of his personality or gender, and more as an effect of being in proximity to mean girls. Romantic relationships in *Gossip Girl* regularly engage in the simple exchange of economic or social capital for affection, but those relationships, such as between Blair and Nate (Chace Crawford), Serena and Gabriel (Armie Hammer), or Bree (Joanna Garcia) and Nate, lack both affective authenticity and longevity. As I hope to make clear, the romance between Blair and Chuck differs from the courtship between Dan and Serena in quality, intensity, and tenor due to their affective alignment and interest in establishing monogamous commitment.

Dan and Serena's relationship is fraught with various forms of violation and treachery. The fantasy of intertwined relationships and gossip-worthy flings that eventually unveils "the one," a "soulmate," or a "life partner" turns out to be an elaborate conspiracy to get Serena and her world of white prestige to pay attention to the Gatsby-like boy/man behind the curtains, Dan or Lonely Boy. Dan's success in establishing his career as a writer is proportional to his willingness to self-disclose and share details and opinions about his family and friends. After publishing a book, he realizes that anonymity will never bring him the recognition and respect that he thinks he deserves. But, where publishing in his own name offers Dan a kind of power that appears to be earned, anonymity provides him with an unearned power that only he can manipulate. The website Gossip Girl offers Dan access to power that is not hindered by his economic or social class, and it is this kind of unbarred access to and curious fixation on the white bourgeois feminine body that attracts the characters to participate in the Gossip Girl site.[19] Like Twitter, Facebook, and TikTok, where celebrities can interact with fans, Gossip Girl disrupts that distancing between the somebodies and the nobodies, the haves and the have-nots, by providing exclusive information about white bourgeois social spaces. Still, having information that could compromise a person's image and credibility is dubbed by the characters as "owning" someone, and becomes a goal in order to have "power over" someone. The information from Gossip Girl's posts is weaponized so that Dan can "own" the girls or women he falls in love with. In his intention to show Blair's character and Serena's allure, he subjects them to unnecessary scrutiny, shaming them for their choices, and objectifying them. His middle-classness operates as a naive moralizing force that various characters (Nate, Blair, Chuck) seek out, and ultimately mitigates the hostile appearance of envy. Gossip Girl animates Dan's desire to expose Serena and her white bourgeois world, to which he does not belong. Whereas revealing Blair's charm is met with unrequited love, uncovering Serena's charisma is met with mutual affection, which is affirmed by Serena's proclamation in the final episode that Gossip Girl is a "love letter" to her. Serena's requited love and her eventual understanding of the Gossip Girl site as a "love letter" become retroactive consent to Dan's acts of violation, reframing them as not violent and not in vain. Wanting to be seen as equal to her, Dan too supports Serena in a way that she never articulated, but appears grateful for after the fact. Thus, the violence of his patriarchal manipulation through social media is not a transgression of the feminization of meanness but, instead, an expression of love. Dan and Serena are a kind of compound subject of feminist heterosociality, but the friction caused by Dan's class envy delays their professional alignment and frustrates their affective calibration until their nuptials in the epilogue.

Having declared their affection for each other early on in the show, Blair and Chuck develop a gradual courtship and mutual affective expression, which is calculated and calibrated in relation to their readiness for monogamy. As Naomi R. Johnson suggests, "acts of consumption to prepare for romantic relationships are the primary focus of [teen romance] rather than the relationships themselves."[20] Although consummated through sexual intercourse, their relationship buds with hate in the first two seasons, as they try to deny and reject any positive feeling or care toward the other and instead compete to hurt, upset, and injure the other. Whether Blair and Chuck's sabotages are enough is determined by whether they can one-up each other's inflicted injuries (or, at the very least, evenly match them). However, Ngai explains that envy is "a form of deproprietorization or theft in which the envier robs the object of what it possesses," but that "the real source of antagonism is less the object than idealization itself."[21] Whereas the plot of season 2 consists of a playful tug-of-war where the one who says "I love you" first is the one who also concedes, season 3 is a series of games where Blair and Chuck humiliate potential love interests for encroaching on their monogamous relationship while at the same time seeking out objects, opportunities, and transactions that further their entrepreneurial selves. These games are an illustration of how imitation and identification organize affective expression to show love's depth, to demonstrate the lengths one might go to, and to set the boundaries between self-worth and togetherness. Their envious aggression culminates in destruction with season 3's dramatic ending. Chuck trades sex with Blair to regain his hotel from his uncle and then, after a fight with Blair, sleeps with Blair's biggest nemesis, a climax in their conflict that is only resolved through a contract that divides assets, territories, and social functions. By treating their romance as a separate domain that infringes on their professional and social lives, Blair and Chuck jeopardize any commitment to monogamy and therefore their relationship.

Their relationship does not mature until Blair and Chuck realize how to sync up their career interests with their social and cultural capital—that is, until their envy transitions from destruction to affiliation. Indeed, the power couple's professional alignment with their social and personal spheres is a common trope for North American entertainment in the neoliberal era: appearing in action films *Mr. & Mrs. Smith* (2005) and *Salt* (2010); romantic comedies like *Keeping Up with the Joneses* (2016), *One Fine Day* (1996), and *Friends with Benefits* (2011); and even in children's animated films like *Ratatouille* (2007). This common trope of professional alignment coalesces with feminist values of self-determination and gender awareness in other popular movies, like *Legally Blonde* (2001), *How to Lose a Guy in 10 Days* (2003), *No Strings Attached* (2011), *What Women Want* (2000), and *The Ugly Truth* (2009). For Blair and Chuck to transform their envy from its destructive tendencies to a coordinated heterosociality, their romantic maturation involves turning away from the violence and betrayal that marked the early stages of the relationship and their early selves, especially Chuck's attempted rapes of Serena and Jenny. Interestingly, the actor who plays Chuck, Ed Westwick, claims that his character was inspired by Patrick Bateman (Christian Bale) from *American Psycho* (2000), a character who is marred with envy.[22] Chuck's predatory behavior is dismissed as frivolous and recedes from the show's drama as Blair's readiness for monogamy with Chuck comes into focus.

For Blair and Chuck, the delay in monogamy comes from each partner's wish to become established and successful in business in their own right. In this interim period of making and preparing their entrepreneurial selves, both Blair and Chuck express love toward the other by helping advance the other's business goals. It is when Blair and Chuck deploy their capital and resources, social networks, and energies with passionate, total disregard for the effects that their love toward each other appears most genuine, deep, and authentic. This tension between the self-regulating subject and the constraints that marriage and monogamy present to that self-regulation is negotiated through the drama involving Chuck's power-hungry patriarch, Bart (Robert John Burke), who retakes control of Bass Industries because Bart claims that Chuck's devotion to Blair clouded his economic judgment. While North American heterosexist culture is invested in constructing marriage as a trap, it is through the concept of the white power couple that neoliberal capitalism offers to smooth over cultural contradictions. Over the course of the show, Blair and Chuck discover that their partner's ideas and strengths are advantageous to their professional ventures, and when Blair and Chuck agree to team up to take down Bart, Bart falls to his death. To guarantee that even the law cannot interfere in the commitment between Blair and Chuck (by forcing Blair to testify about how Bart died and risk incriminating Chuck), Blair and Chuck get married at the series' conclusion.

The accusations of attempted rape and sexual harassment that haunt Chuck (like Westwick himself, after the series ended) never disturb Blair or disrupt the audience's concern for Blair's continued relationship with him: this is because her safety is protected by mean girl feminism's commitment to monogamous love.[23] Since Chuck's predations occur before their relationship or are assumed to happen outside of it, Blair's demonstrations of love gauge his capacity for atonement. When Blair rejects Chuck, their relationship status serves as a measure of how destructive and violent Chuck will be, and likewise, when Blair accepts Chuck, it shows how her intimacy prevents him from violence. Though different relations of violence and power are at play, other movies and series, like *Fifty Shades of Grey* (2015–18) and *The Twilight Saga* (2008–12), similarly position the mean girl of the power couple to save and redeem the violent white man.[24]

If Blair's desire for self-regulation and autonomy is viewed as central to *Gossip Girl*'s narrative action, the narrativized making of the white power couple presents Chuck's continued support of Blair through the difficulties of negotiating among domestic, professional, and social spheres. Whereas

Blair's efforts to support him mostly backfire (e.g., locating an alcohol license for Chuck's speakeasy), Chuck is more successful in his efforts, which are dedicated to winning her over and take place in the public eye (making visible the messy drama that is obscured in the case of the Clintons, whom I discuss next). How Chuck earns her affection and redeems himself from the violence he causes is part of the show's very appeal of centering a power couple who desperately tries to have it all, against all odds and all conventions. To repair his character, Chuck overcompensates by overidentifying with her. Chuck changes from predatory playboy to scheming lover, adopting Blair's distinctive mode of mean girl problem-solving. Rigging her prom queen win, applying to Columbia University on her behalf, and orchestrating her first fashion show while she suffers from exhaustion, Chuck is always one step ahead of her because he knows what she wants without it ever being articulated. Considering that Blair tries to similarly forecast his desire but fails, feminist envy celebrates Blair as a model for Chuck to imitate. Thus, out of all the mean girls whom Blair has tried to outwit, reign over, and wrangle into her girl squad, Chuck is Blair's best minion. Through his actions of becoming like her or becoming hers, they become a kind of compound subject of feminist heterosociality. His imitation affects Blair, helping her appreciate that monogamous coupledom can be mobilized as an extension of herself and that cis-heteropatriarchy offers her the conditions of possibility to become the girlboss she wants to be. His acts of love transform him into a future version of Blair, suggesting not just his devotion, but also his potential to be a thoughtful subject of feminism. With Chuck's violent masculinity receding into the background, power coupledom through Chuck's mimesis becomes the site of feminist agency. In *Gossip Girl*, mean girl performativity produces feminist compoundedness through the power couple, by using the white woman as the exemplar through which cis-heteropatriarchy can refound itself.

Mean Girl's Unrequited Love

While a television series like *Gossip Girl* shows the daily drama of performing as a power couple, political marriages have tried to wrangle control over their image and impression. The traditional nuclear family has been deployed as an icon of good moral judgment that intimates conservative political stances against taxes, feminism, and multicultural difference.[25] Public figures, particularly white men, utilize "family values" to give the impression of marital harmony and a solid domestic life. Given that racial endogamy (marriage within the same race) is still the most common practice, white politicians may be utilizing photo and media opportunities to convey an image of racial loyalty as well.[26]

The enduring presence of power couples can suggest that there is more to politics than meets the eye. In antiquity, ancient power couples or "imperial couples" mobilized their family and social networks to support the art of governing.[27] When Hillary and Bill Clinton entered the scene of government and politics, they became one of the first power couples "in which both parents work, and in which to a great degree, the marriage itself is seen as work."[28] Not far from this logic that relationships are forms of labor is an argument put forward by scholars Patrick Jones and Gretchen Soderlund, who observe that power couples on television are embedded in interpersonal relationships fraught with conspiracy, scandal, schemes, and ambition. That the interpersonal realm moves politics in asymmetrical directions, toward and around political power couples, is not the exception but the rule. This interpersonal economy marks a new ontology or "conspiratorial mode": "the very substance of politics itself as opposed to a deviation from politics as usual."[29] Homing in on the shrewdness attributed to the female half of power couples, Suzanne Leonard argues that Hillary Clinton is "the *sine qua non* of political wifedom," the "suffering wife" whose "image of resilience . . . ground[s] portrayals of political wives, and set[s] new terms by which such figures claim agency, often by making their own stab at a political candidacy."[30] This conspiratorial mode shapes how the women are often viewed as pushy goal (if not gold) diggers and mean girls, even while their partners engage in unethical behavior with little to no repercussion. The news media too has adopted this mode of thinking, with American political power couples subjected to more public scrutiny than celebrities or private individuals. The *Washington Monthly* chronicles concern about "power-couple syndrome" back to 1994, which prompted calls for clear rules around conflict of interest.[31] Whereas the notion of family values connotes trustworthiness and morality for political men, feminist analyses of power couples suggest that it can have the opposite effect for political women, whose marital and familial life can be met with political cynicism and accusations of transactional relationships. Although family values mobilize the private sphere as another resource for imperialism and white supremacy, feminism attributes the failure of family values to work for white women's embourgeoisement to sex-binary discrimination.

Dubbed "America's ultimate power couple," Hillary and Bill Clinton have been public figures since Bill ran for a seat on the House of Representatives in 1974.[32] The idea that they were a power couple gained traction with Bill's first presidential bid, in 1992, when he campaigned with the catchphrase that voters could get "two for one": him in the presidency, and Hillary at his side as wife, political adviser, and supporter. However, when Hillary was asked tough questions about her husband's workplace behavior and sexual harassment, her cold demeanor hinted that voters would be met with evasive answers and dodging about the power couple's affection for each other. As Loren Glass puts it, "Everyone knows what Bill and Monica did, but the nature of intimate relations between Bill and Hillary Clinton remains open to speculation."[33] Scholar Melissa Deem questions feminists like Betty Friedan and Patricia Ireland, who came to Bill's defense and support the familial logic that tolerates male indiscretion, and wonders whether for women "the complexities of the workplace and the political sphere are reduced to the intimate confines of the heterosexual and hence private marriage, the most sacred of all personal domains."[34] Similarly, Kate O'Beirne opines in the *National Review* that "Bill Clinton's ultimate fate is thought to rest with a jury of one" (i.e., Hillary), who will declare that he is "fit for marriage" and that his "'just sex' offenses [can be neatly placed inside] the private sphere of their bizarre marriage."[35] On the one hand, the model that Hillary sets for power couples could be encouraging for feminists seeking bipartisan progress with conservatives.[36] On the other hand, however, as commentator Erica Jong concludes, this inconsistency between the publicness of the power couple and the privateness of their love (to which the public seems to feel entitled) points to the "conventional rather than revolutionary" aspects of their power coupledom, for "it's the female half that gets trashed while the male half is forgiven for all his transgressions and winds up being President. Bill Clinton owes Hillary. Big."[37] Thus, the story of Hillary as the wronged wife cuts twice over: wronged by his sexual offenses, and wronged by the public's refusal to accept her because of it.

The story of the wronged wife becomes part of the narrative of *Hillary* (2020), a four-part documentary series directed by Nanette Burstein that was made available on Hulu and Netflix after premiering at film festivals. Aimed at providing a comprehensive understanding of Hillary as a public figure who is both hated and loved, the documentary series chronicles Hillary's life from her childhood to her 2016 presidential loss, featuring interviews with and accounts from friends, politicians, and reporters. In an early memory that bears similarity to Joreen's recollections of the civil rights movement as inspiration for her feminist writings (see chapter 1), Hillary recalls and credits Dr. Martin Luther King Jr.'s speech about waking up to injustice as helping her to recognize sexism when she lost to a boy in a run for class president. Again, she segues from the white violence of the 1960s to gender inequity. Sexism becomes the main frame through which Hillary's appeal among women—and the antifeminist and conservative hatred toward her—is to be understood. The documentary recounts various sexist incidents that have affected her career and likability: from her choice to drop her maiden name and soften her look for Bill's Arkansas gubernatorial campaign in 1978, to her gendered frustrations of the 2016 presidential race: the hours dedicated to makeup and clothing, the sexist comments made by her opponent.

While the documentary is named for Hillary and centered on her life, it is Bill's career as a politician that seems to create her working conditions and social visibility: clips from her gubernatorial campaigning on his behalf to bring out women voters; his presidential slogan of "Buy one, get one free"; her legal experience on the Nixon impeachment and consequent opposition to Bill's impeachment; and her interviews supporting Bill after revelations about Monica Lewinsky. Through her devotion to the body politic, here also the metaphorical and physical body of the sovereign, Hillary appears to be nothing more than Bill's double. While the feminist framing of the documentary illustrates her failed presidential run as rooted in sexism, I want to suggest that her defense of her husband's questionable sexual behavior is the very cause of the sexism that drives potential voters away. Clips abound of then presidential candidate Donald Trump noting that Hillary is married to a man who abuses women, commentators speculating that a right-wing conspiracy would lie about anything to limit the Clintons' success, and campaign managers discussing focus groups who questioned why she stayed in her marriage even though they would vote for Bill again if given the opportunity. While it is clear that her life's work has been focused on centering women, Hillary also seems to presume that her feminism does not have bearing on her relationship with Bill, and allows her to refuse questions and concerns about her alignment with white male violence—as is evident in the way she evades questions and refuses to be accountable about her intimate relationship with Bill. Feminism appears to be a tool that is convenient for Hillary's embourgeoisement and disarticulated to the power relations that her relationship with Bill enables.

Although sexism is the white feminist frame of the *Hillary* narrative, ending with her failed presidential campaign and its spawning of a feminist revival of sorts, what remains unexplained and left to public wonderment is whether and how Bill has reconciled with Hillary and whether such efforts are satisfactory. This curious uncertainty about whether their relationship structure is open, loving, or genuine brings to mind the words of Lauren Berlant: "Everyone knows what the female complaint is: women live for love, and love is the gift that keeps on taking."[38] Their life together is no Blair and Chuck love story arc, with love bombing and grand, highly visible attempts by Bill to win Hillary's heart back; and as the documentary makes clear, Hillary is said to hold the belief that she has "dealt with" the problems of her marriage and that everyone else should move on. (Huma Abedin—vice chair of Hillary's 2016 campaign and someone who is "like a daughter" to her—would follow the same model in her marriage to former congressperson and convicted sex offender Anthony Weiner.) Thus, while Hillary rescued Bill's character and is the undeniable heroine of the Clinton administration, the underlying question of whether he deserved her rescue remains unanswered and unsaid.

The Clintons are a power couple that operates from a selective application of the feminist principle that the personal is political. Bill's deployment of Hillary for his campaign and politics follows this feminist principle more than Hillary's campaign and politics, which keep her relationship with Bill as separate from her public image and politics. On one level, the kind of compound subject of feminist heterosociality that is Hillary and Bill appears to be a professional alliance, in which Bill benefits more than Hillary. Through his relationship with Hillary, Bill can center gender and make the feminine/subject a characteristic from which to borrow. At another level, in vying to become president and refusing to talk publicly about her relationship with Bill, Hillary appears to be motivated by envy (that, she wants to be like him or a future him: a sovereign), and she bears the brunt of that hostility. By not making her personal sphere political, Hillary evades the inverse relationship between violence and intimacy that is naturalized in white male violence. Hillary is the bad example of feminism's cooperation with cis-heteropatriarchy and, paradoxically, also cis-heteropatriarchy's best subject—working for it, empowering it, loving it, and rescuing it from and because of its faults.

Conclusion

Power couple feminism modernizes cis-heteropatriarchy, making it a terrain for feminist heterosociality by appropriating the strategies and feelings of working in solidarity with others for the woman's own efforts at coupledom and family. By positioning her other as male and reinscribing the sex binary, the mean girl feminist proves that she can work with (male) difference and still accomplish goals. Power couple feminism shows how the site of neoliberal success is not limited to the individual subject and can be located in coupledom. At first glance, the power couple's romance evokes the feminist goal of having it all: the mean girl with her mean antics can be loved and can get her happily ever after of monogamous romance and professional empire.

However, a closer analysis takes notice of how envy restructures the violent white man's hopeless devotion as a source of redemption, a kind of salvation that is not utilized by or available to Bill and Hillary Clinton.

With Bill and Chuck each situated as part of a power couple, violence is normalized within feminist heterosociality; it is the cost of loving and being in love with white men. The inverse relationship between violence and intimacy functions as the barometer of love's presence and as the cause of white men's violent spirals. Power couple feminism checks and balances male violence rather than opposing it. From this perspective, the power couple feminist is a better kind of master for white supremacy because she can discern white male violence and is the source of its eventual redemption. Her continued relationship with violent white men along with her feminism gaslight claims about that very violence.

Having shown how power couple feminism restructures white women's sovereignty in the matters of romantic love, I turn in chapter 4 to the topic of family, to consider the relationship between global motherhood, feminism, and biopower. Of interest is how global motherhood, the idea that the white global mother can help create a multicultural global family, coalesces with conservative feminism in ways that mitigate ideological antagonisms and allow for the expansion of white biopower.

CHAPTER 4

GLOBAL MOTHER FEMINISM

Gatekeeping Biopower and Sovereignty

"We take motherhood for granted sometimes," Elena Richardson (Reese Witherspoon) says in *Little Fires Everywhere* (2020), a miniseries based on Celeste Ng's 2017 eponymous book about the interracial dynamics of the small town of Shaker Heights, Ohio, in the 1990s. Here, Elena is sharing a glass of wine with Mia Warren (Kerry Washington), and it is a rare moment of bonding in which Elena intends her comment to compliment Mia's parenting and relationship with her child while alluding to Elena's troubled relationship with her own queer daughter. But her use of *we* is odd. In her performance of the put-together white feminist woman, Elena does take motherhood for granted, but it becomes less obvious that Mia and others do so as well. If her compliment to Mia is meant as genuine, it is made strange by Elena's competitiveness and her performance of global motherhood throughout the series. Elena not only offers Mia employment but, as her landlord as well, Elena negotiates terms of the lease. Elena insists on "helping" Mia's daughter, Pearl (Lexi Underwood), by feeding her, assisting her with a letter to the counselor, and getting her out of trouble. Elena's insistence on doing good on Pearl's behalf allows her to avoid dealing with the realization that her own child is queer, and avoid noticing that her "perfect" daughter stole Pearl's experience for an admission essay and used Pearl's name to get an abortion. Global motherhood also pervades the storyline of undocumented Chinese immigrant Bebe Chow (Huang Lu) and her legal struggle with Elena's white friend Linda McCullough (Rosemarie DeWitt), who is trying to adopt Chow's baby. When McCullough wins her legal battle, the town is divided along racial lines and the metaphor of superior white motherhood unravels when Elena is forced to reckon with the truth about her marriage and family just as her house burns down.

I open with this vignette and summary of the series because *Little Fires Everywhere* could be read as a parable of white fragility when the savior role of white woman comes into crisis. More specifically, global mother feminism gatekeeps white efforts to do good, operationalizing them as feminist acts that can serve as an antidote to their own white colonial aggression.[1] As Lauren Berlant has argued, "Embedded in the often sweetly motivated and solidaristic activity of the intimate public of femininity is a white universalist paternalism, sometimes dressed as maternalism."[2] Feminism enables a popular shift within white supremacy from white men to white women, who offer moral leadership and renew confidence in the colonial nation-state. Ruby Hamad puts it succinctly: "White women were able to access a form of limited power through maternalistic intervention" into the lives of the colonized through the figuration of the Great White Mother.[3] Global motherhood figures white women as productive contributors to Western civilization through their mothering of would-be citizens. Focusing on Princess Diana, Angelina Jolie, Madonna, and other celebrities who serve as UN goodwill ambassadors, Raka Shome describes how the white global mother "becomes a transcendental, trans-spatial, figure who overcomes borders of history, nation, and culture while also silently re-inscribing them in new ways through an affective politics of love and family that is writ large on the contemporary global landscape of despair and poverty." Shome explains that global motherhood "circulates familial desires that shore up white heterosexual patriarchal kinship structures and in doing so erase the masculinist violence of western colonialisms that have destroyed familial domesticities in so many nations in the global south."[4] Global motherhood is applicable to a range of Western imperial actions: from eugenicist campaigns about preserving racial traits and raising good biological stock with all-white families, to segregationist crusades for selective and revisionist history in public school textbooks, to the erection of post–American Civil War mammy memorials to "remember the best friend of their childhood."[5] My understanding of global motherhood also follows Louise Michele Newman's argument that "imperialism provided an important discourse for white elite women who developed new identities for themselves as missionaries, explorers, educators, and ethnographers as they staked out new realms of possibility and political power against tight constraints of Victorian gender norms."[6] Global mother feminism feminizes colonial biopower by positioning women as principled sovereigns who perform white maternalism.

I turn to global mother feminism as a kind of mean girl feminism to theorize how global motherhood has been taken up by feminists as deserving of solidarity and defense against sexism. In addition, the difference between liberal and conservative feminists is reconciled in global mother feminism, which shifts away from a rights-based political platform and toward a performativity embodied by white heteronormative motherhood. As Rafia Zakaria explains, "the terrible plight of foreign women who did not have their rights and privileges . . . was the bipartisan issue that allowed white feminists of different political affiliations to speak to each other."[7] I examine two instances—one involving First Lady Laura Bush, and the other involving vice presidential candidate Sarah Palin—where feminists argued that a woman's political leadership was undermined by sexist ignorance about women's well-being and their historical exclusion. Through her role as First Lady, Bush reconstructed the War on Terror as "America's first 'feminist' war," an international initiative that offered biopolitical advantages for Afghan women.[8] As Kyla Schuller explains, "White feminism works within biopolitics, rather than against it, to carve out a prominent place for middle-class women within these fatal dynamics."[9] First Lady Bush transformed her husband's rhetoric about invasion and the use of brute force against al-Qaeda and Osama bin Laden by constituting the International War on Terror as a liberal, humanitarian mission to provide Afghan women with educational and business opportunities. Whereas Bush was seen as a nice lady who attracted moderate and liberal support to the Republican Party, Sarah Palin's meanness became a hallmark of the aggressive rhetoric and practices that splintered the Republican Party and that paved the way for President Donald Trump's polarizing approach to politics. Known to spread vicious gossip about her opponents or naysayers and to call on her associates to lie, Palin openly used bigotry and prejudicial language to advocate for a conservative program against government regulations.[10] Although one was genial and the other polarizing, both Bush and Palin expanded white biopower through their performance of global motherhood, which provoked feminist defense of their work. In global mother feminism, the undervalued woman, whether in the United States or Afghanistan, poses a biopolitical threat to the longevity of the population, civilization, democracy, and other hailed ideas of the West. While diverging in tone and word choice in white saviorism and colonial aggression, both Bush and Palin promote gratitude for the fact of not being other, pity for those who are other, and, simultaneously, hatred for "the underlying conditions of their nations."[11]

This chapter, then, explores how Sarah Palin and Laura Bush each perform global motherhood, which feminism protects in its commitment to the sex binary and womanhood. By minimizing antagonism toward politically conservative white women, feminism eases embourgeoisement and expands white biopower's capacity to determine care and quality of life in statecraft. Moreover, global motherhood appropriates the empowerment rhetoric that began as a tactic of South Asian grassroots feminism and distorts it into white feminism.[12] As a result of the gendered alignment and reduced antagonism between white conservative feminists and white liberal feminists, feminism strengthens racial lines and facilitates the mainstreaming of white conservativism. Global mother feminists are better, nicer masters because they imbue white biopower with the moral ethos and performativity of gender for white women. In so doing, global mother feminists contribute to gaslighting, portraying imperialist white supremacist capitalist cis-heteropatriarchy as nonviolent and progressive.

Sarah Palin as Global Mother

Like with her 1996 electoral campaign for the mayorship of Wasilla, Alaska, Sarah Palin's national emergence in 2008 was notable for her campaign's divisive orientation around identity. In Wasilla she campaigned on her born-again Christian faith, focused less on what to do about potholes and more on who politicians and their constituents were (once in office, she fired department heads who had voted against her); on the national scene, she similarly created clear allies and enemies. In addition to promoting the War on Terror as a needed act of violent aggression, Palin spread fear with unverified claims such as that Barack Obama was "palling around with terrorists."[13] Espousing both conservative and liberal ideals and often doing so without much explanation or elaboration, Palin took inconsistent and incoherent stances on a range of issues from abortion and welfare (she was opposed to both) to corporate taxes and Title IX (for which she was in favor). The most consistent element of her politics would seem to be a steadfast commitment to individual self-interest and biopolitical self-determination. After Palin's running mate, John McCain, lost to Obama, Palin became a Fox News commentator (2010–13), penned a memoir on the campaign (the 2009 *Going Rogue*), and had a one-season reality television show called *Sarah Palin's Alaska* (2010–11) on the TLC network—all of which continued to provide her with a platform for meanness that trafficked in racist sentiment and middle- and lower-class resentment.[14] In fact, *Going Rogue*—which was named after the way Senator McCain's staffers described Palin's off-script comments and was written with the help of ghostwriter Lynn Vincent—spent weeks at the top of the New York Times Best Seller List, and two of her next three books would also be named bestsellers. As Joanna Weiss commented about Palin's charisma, "Being a mommy sells policy. Being a mean girl sells books."[15]

Palin's political inconsistency is smoothed over by her positionality and use of gender as a category for analysis: gender, not whiteness, became an important topos for interpreting Palin's political base and overall appeal. Ruth Rosen reports that "between a third and a half of Tea Party activists are female," and she quotes one emphatic participant: "In the Tea Party, women have finally found their voice."[16] Conversely, Linda Hirshman notes that men made up most of Sarah Palin's fan base.[17] Wendy Anderson affirms Palin's gender performativity in becoming the "de facto head of the Tea Party": "Sarah Palin embodies a white 'maternal feminist' identity, which offers and eagerly invites white women to a seat at the political table."[18] In this section, I analyze how Palin's performance of global motherhood as a self-described mama grizzly bear coincides with her persona as a mean girl feminist participating in electoral politics.

Palin's campaign as a mean girl feminist was no different from other American electoral campaigns, to the extent that meanness helps voters distinguish the ethoi of candidates and fosters name recognition for those politicians. Intrusive background checks, interviews with neighbors and associates, reportage of previous policy decisions or stances, and outing of personal affairs are considered par for the course for those with political ambitions. Voters often vote on politicians' character and credibility—their "competing ethoi"—not policies, and "base their candidate choice and partisan identification on how they feel about other blocs of voters and the connections they perceive between political candidates and particular groups or interests in society."[19] Although scholars have conceptualized this political meanness in pejorative ways (e.g., as muckraking and dirty tricks), Bruce E. Gronbeck argues that the elements of meanness found in campaigns, elections, and politics should be understood as "negative narratives" because they succeed in suggesting to constituents that the opponent has poor judgment and makes bad decisions.[20] In fact, verbal ruthlessness exhibited in negative narratives is interpreted as a positive quality of leadership, one that shows an ability to get the job done and an honest willingness to unmask concerns about an opponent's character. Situating negative narrative within the broad ad-like form of public communication that has been popularized on television, Kathleen Hall Jamieson argues that assertion and attack, instead of argument and critical engagement, have become the norm. She explains that televised campaigns gain access to low-involvement viewers who receive only incidental exposure to political information and are more likely to be persuaded by attractiveness or "peripheral cues" of the candidate.[21] Since evidence or factuality is taken in this context as secondary to assertiveness and rightness, Arthur H. Miller and Bruce E. Gronbeck claim: "Institutional constraints aside, majority support for a candidate occurs largely because the winning candidate successfully devised a set of messages aimed at evoking or representing the shared fears and hopes of the electorate."[22] One of the first well-known negative narratives in a political campaign was put forth in 1988 by Republican presidential candidate George H. W. Bush (then vice president) against his Democratic opponent, Michael Dukakis (then the governor of Massachusetts). This negative narrative stoked racial fear by broadcasting the 1986 case of Willie Horton, a Black man who, while serving prison time in Massachusetts (convicted of murder) had received a weekend furlough—only to flee the state and commit rape, assault, and robbery on a white couple in Maryland. Bush's campaign stoked racial fear and appealed to white values, warning that a Dukakis win would mean a "revolving door" in the nation's prisons.[23] Gronbeck and others observe that negative narratives not only solidify racial and class lines but also remind constituents that governmental processes are subject to and even absolved by human shortcomings.[24] Contrary to the popular belief that political missteps hurt politicians and their careers, factual inaccuracies, gaffes, and politically incorrect terms rarely harm the speaker's character; this is "because the rhetors are dealing with generalities and wisdom rather than with details and knowledge."[25] Thus, negativity, including fake news and lies, has been part of the political campaign trail since at least the late 1980s, and Palin's role in reproducing a negative narrative is consistent rather than at odds with electoral norms.

However, commentators and scholars have focused on the role of gender as unique to Palin's appeal, both positively and negatively. Diplomatic eloquence, logical organization, and deliberative argument are all discursive privileges afforded to seasoned political elite. Palin stood in stark contrast here—and for this her gender was seen as to blame. Newspaper commentator Maureen Dowd worried, for example, that Palin's gendered appeal makes ignorance trendy.[26] Laurie Ouellette similarly admits, "Palin's enduring visibility since the 2008 election evidences a strategic mastery of both old and new media forms."[27] The play between ignorance and a sense of mastery leads Jeffrey Broxmeyer to argue that Palin enacts infantile citizenship, which describes Reaganite-era complacency toward (and concomitant lack of knowledge about) state affairs and deploys white, bourgeois, heterosexual family-oriented values.[28] Palin's gendered popularity seemed to pose a crisis to electoral politics and to white women's visibility.

When Palin was subjected to criticism, both conservative and liberal feminists came to her defense, culminating in liberal Melissa McEwan's launch of the blog post series Sarah Palin Sexism Watch.[29] In a *New York*

Times opinion piece, Anna Holmes and Rebecca Traister noted that liberal feminists disapproved of Palin's shrewd opportunism and meanness and were relegating her politics to postfeminism.[30] Elsewhere, Traister suggested that despite Palin's performance of traditional womanhood (which Traister would normally be one to oppose), media coverage of Tea Party candidates like Palin was selective and the overall negative image of women politicians was due to a sexist media.[31] In response to liberal feminists who did criticize Palin, Colleen Carroll Campbell opined that the unfair criticism of Palin originated from "America's feminist establishment," which views feminism within a narrow frame of "sisterhood" and solidarity.[32] Kathleen Parker argued that modern-day feminism and "sisterhood" should accept that there will be women politicians with whom some women simply do not agree.[33]

What Dowd, McEwan, Holmes, Traister, Campbell, and Parker point to is how Palin's candidacy activated a conversation among white feminists about feminist performativity and about whose performance can be said to be enduring sexism. While I do not deny that gender plays a role in the way in which negative narrative may play out for women versus men in politics, the scholars and commentators above emphasize Palin's emergence as a gendered outsider to the current forms of governmentality, rather than critiquing how feminism itself fueled public fascination with white feminine performance. Indeed, feminist fascination with the white feminine body is reinforced in Tina Fey's impression of Palin on *Saturday Night Live*, which attributed Palin's popularity to her attractiveness. In my view of situating Palin's meanness as negative narrative, Palin's conservative politics and performance do not put electoral politics in crisis; nor do they reinvent feminism or gender analysis. Palin mobilizes global motherhood as conservative and ordinary feminism for her (s)kinfolk.

In *Going Rogue*, Palin recounts how her gender as a politician was undervalued: from the McCain campaign's handling and advice, to her 2008 appearance on *Saturday Night Live*, to her political disputes as shaped by "liberal" mainstream media and politicians—or the "professional political caste"—who value "scripted nonanswers." Referring to public service as a "politics of personal destruction," Palin narrates her entry into politics as provoked by shady Big Oil, crooked government deals, and "good ol' boys"— a phrase that appears again and again to refer to anyone from corrupt liberals to established Republican politicians to women-hating sexists.[34] Throughout *Going Rogue*, she describes her role in the McCain campaign as hamstrung by the Republican National Committee, and her media presence as hampered by a "hostile press," media misinformation, and poor research on the part of journalists.[35] Over and over, Palin discusses how she was silenced by the McCain campaign or violated its protocol, how she was excluded from decision-making processes associated with the campaign, and how her most articulate moments were cut from her interview with Katie Couric.[36] Full of corruption and liberal elitism, the public sphere is hostile to the unprepped, real, and rogue Palin because, according to her memoir, she is not liberal and she is not a man. Part of this gendered political terrain, Palin's memoir and her attack campaigns establish an us-versus-them binary (with "them" including her challengers and foreign others alike) that intensifies racial pride for her global mother feminism. Antiestablishment cowboys versus elite, educated Yankees, and the Republican haves versus the Democratic have-nots: this binary shows her perspective of historical and structural antagonisms and her desire for white belonging and unity.[37] Palin's neoliberal rhetoric of decentralized government and respect for Second Amendment rights, along with the references to "states' rights," "law and order," and "individual rights," are coded words and phrases for white supremacist values.[38] Zakaria explains: "As white feminists have progressed within their societies and begun to occupy increasingly important positions, they are constructing a feminism that uses the lives of Black and Brown people as arenas in which they can prove their credentials to white men."[39] Thus, Palin's negative narrative may not clarify her policies and formulate deliberative argumentation, but it does situate her within a white vernacular that ascribes the politics of love, family, and unity from global mother feminism with whiteness.

Thus, it is against a white feminist backdrop that Palin justifies her political pursuit as "true public service" and as a biopolitical exercise of care for the people of the small town of Wasilla, the state of Alaska, and the nation.[40] Historically, white women have secured a basic quality of life for themselves, their white men, and their white children, by building "political platforms that translated political support for white supremacy into broader debates on national sovereignty, genocide, and the fate of developing nations."[41] Palin has been described as a "supermom" to her five children, and her family is seen as illustrative of her capacity to care and exercise love for the biopolitical health of the nation.[42] While Princess Diana, Madonna, and others might be prototypes of global motherhood and its cross-border liberal charm, Palin too performs global motherhood: she just does so with a tenor of meanness that centers white love as both means and ends for global mother feminism.

If the global mother invokes white purity in an effort to promote global love for the other stricken by colonial violence, then Palin asserts a notion of global motherhood that affirms white American patriotism as a form of protection for the nation and the globe. As a "fiercely protective good mother"—"a cultural designation reserved exclusively for white, middle- and upper-class women"—Palin self-identifies as a "mama grizzly bear," something that comes across in her affective politics of love for the family, the nation, and the world.[43] In 2007, as Alaska governor, Palin selected Alaska's state quarter design to carry the image of a grizzly bear hunting salmon because the grizzly was "doing what she does best: taking care of her young."[44] According to Wendy Anderson, "Palin capitalized on the acceptable privilege of aggression of [white] moms through her articulation of mama grizzlies."[45] Palin has used the term to promote the Alaska natural gas pipeline project when her son was about to be deployed to Iraq, to underscore the challenges of her being in the public eye for her family and children, and to label political candidates whose platforms she approved of.[46] The notion of the "mama grizzly bear" enables Palin to position herself as a global mother who not only urges love for one's family and the American nation-state, but also evokes a neoliberal logic that extends care of self and family to care for the other and the globe.

Palin's mean antics are part of the political script of demonstrating character and celebrity in a field of public service dictated by marketing and public relations principles. Gronbeck distinguishes between character and celebrity, arguing that character has a moral dimension that Aristotle crafted in his tripartite description of ethos, while celebrity is the ability to spin any experience or episode of one's life into "an index of cultural life, a generalization to be seized, a lesson to be learned."[47] Gronbeck's distinction between character and celebrity points to a tension in feminism that Palin exposes: the display of character as moral, on the one hand, versus the gendered display of celebrity as spun into "an index of cultural life," on the other. But identifying with gender without partaking in structural analysis that also accounts for white supremacy works similarly to how white feminists use the term *privileged*: "more like a transparency measure rather than an incentive to engage further."[48] Palin's performance of mean girl feminism illustrates global motherhood as an apparatus of imperialist white supremacist capitalist cis-heteropatriarchy.

Laura Bush as Global Mother

Interestingly, First Lady Laura Bush was seen, much like Sarah Palin, as an exceptional conservative, but for entirely different reasons. With a popularity rating higher than her husband's and a fundraising capacity for other politicians that outpaced most Republicans, First Lady Bush played an important role in capturing the moderate and liberal vote by propagandizing the post-9/11 War on Terror in Afghanistan and campaigning for her husband's second term in 2004.[49] She was called the "hidden asset" of the George W. Bush administration and the "secret weapon" of the Republican Party.[50] Former secretary of state Condoleezza Rice credits the First Lady for her "initiative and her idea to really fully and completely expose what the Taliban regime was doing to women, emphasizing violations of women's rights prior to the U.S. invasion of Afghanistan."[51] Making history by delivering the president's weekly radio address on November 17, 2001, the First Lady created goodwill and promoted confidence in the War on Terror in ways not possible through any other office within the Bush administration. Thus, behind and in front of the White House, it was the First Lady who rationalized the War on Terror in Afghanistan as a liberal war that would better the lives of Afghan women, children, and men. By infusing liberal war with maternalism, Bush's global mother feminism continues a long history of appropriating the empowerment approach conceived of in the 1980s by Indian feminist organization Development Alternatives with Women for a New Era, which aimed to bring about structural change in ways that "white-led, top-down paradigms of development had not delivered."[52]

Liberal war is the idea that war is waged not only to discourage practices that threaten life, but also to guard the production and improvement of life. Although the first family's history with the Saudis and business in oil were seen as underlying motivations for justifying war against the Taliban, the War on Terror was reconstituted as a humanitarian mission to care for Afghan women. Hamad elaborates, "What was missing [in the Bush administration rhetoric] was the historical context of how the Taliban had come to power, and the role that Western powers had played in their rise."[53] Building on Michel Foucault's biopolitics, Michael Dillon and Julian Reid coined the term *liberal war* to reflect how war is no longer figured as a geopolitical struggle over national borders, but is waged to improve the life of the people within a regime.[54] Premised on the governmental protection of subjects through a discourse of equal rights, liberalism claims to achieve peace and prevent economic, social, and political conflict between its subjects by instituting surveillance domestically and waging war internationally. However, Dillon and Reid point out that wars have always been premised on liberal rule and that "the life of the species is wagered on military-political strategies said to advance the cause of peace and prosperity on behalf of the species." Because biopoliticization scrutinizes ways of life that are deemed good or bad for subjects within a regime's governance and constructed peripheries, "preemptive war is a natural corollary of the biopoliticization of the liberal way of war."[55]

The First Lady is well suited to helping the public make sense of the bio-politics of liberal war, and Bush's success at gaslighting in this area—recasting the War on Terror as a feminist biopolitical effort—can be partially credited to the women who came before her in the role of the First Lady as the mother of the nation. The activities of the First Lady are often evaluated in terms of how they reinforce domesticity, and the ideology of motherhood positions the First Lady as an expert on caring for and supporting the well-being of others. Linda Kerber describes how early sexism in the Enlightenment era ascribed civic purpose and duty to the domestic sphere in order to justify the exclusion of women from politics. Modeled off of the Spartan woman who raised her son to sacrifice himself for the polis, republican motherhood celebrates the mother of the republic as serving a political purpose through her dedication to her children and family.[56] Tasha N. Dubriwny explains, "First ladies' rhetoric from the perspective of the rhetorical tradition of the republican mother is both constraining and liberatory, as it confirms women's political role but usually only in the areas of 'women's issues.'"[57] Bush's work as First Lady did not attract as much negative concern as did the advocacy work of her predecessor, Hillary Clinton (which was focused on national health-care reform), because Bush's education policy and literacy initiatives were seen as domestic care for the nation's children.[58] So, when Bush's speeches after 9/11 suggested that the War on Terror ensured education and literacy among girls and women in Afghanistan, Bush was championing mother-hood, earning her the title of "comforter-in-chief."[59] In addition, the fact that Bush had expressed Democratic leanings in her past enhanced the perception that the administration's commitment to the biopolitical management of and care for the population of Afghanistan was a nonpartisan endeavor.[60] The First Lady is subject to different criteria than the president: her role is less about the democratic deliberation of policy, and more about the sustaining of biological life through a centering of nonpolitical and noncontroversial issues.

Having the First Lady, a figure of global motherhood, promote war offers a unique rhetorical advantage for a biopolitical regime. Hamad explains: "White womanhood has functioned as the maternal arm of empire."[61] As an unelected figure, the First Lady is a citizen-subject, but as a public figure, she can function as a liberal subject par excellence. In a state that promises to promote the security of its people and modes of existence, the liberal subject is "constructed by living freely through contingent threats to insecurities around its existence."[62] In order to keep that promise of security, the lib-eral state identifies areas and practices for the calibration and improvement of liberalism's foundations. Brad Evans explains of liberalism's unending emergency, "Every law and every decision respond to an exceptional moment."[63] Thus, the First Lady can speak about the very conditions of emergency and feelings of fear that require the expansion and maintenance of a biopolitical regime from a perspective that is simultaneously *within* and *outside* the administration. Robert P. Watson affirms:

> The first ladyship as an office is an extraconstitutional development. The president's spouse is not mentioned in the Constitution and the position is neither elected nor appointed; as such, it is technically not even an office. However, the first ladies of the modern era have enjoyed office space, a budget, and staff of considerable size, larger than those of most presidential aides and advisers. It is therefore an office but one without portfolio, statutory legitimacy, electoral mandate, or clearly defined roles and responsibilities.[64]

As a liberal subject par excellence who is both within and outside the administration, the First Lady can make arguments without providing the verifiable data that founds her fear, but yet her fear can in turn "become a generative principle of formation for rule."[65] Any factual error made by the First Lady is more or less pardonable because she is unelected, outside of party lines, and not privy to discussions on policy-making. Bush's support of the war appeared to be voluntary and honest, and as an unexpected advocate of the War on Terror, she made "convenient use of the stereotype of women as nonviolent," which enhanced the optics of the war's humanitarian and liberal cause.[66] Furthermore, the tautological logic of gender performance positioned her as a trustworthy figure (that is, because she is a woman, she is not expected to support violence, so, she can be trusted; even though she supports violence in this case, because she is a woman, she can still be trusted). Through her individual past, the history of the office, and her performance, the First Lady was an effective advocate for gaslighting the public on the War on Terror, transforming it into a feminist initiative of global motherhood.

First Lady Bush's global mother feminism constructed the War on Terror as providing infrastructure and education for girls and women, feminist pathways that would lead to independence, entrepreneurship, and resistance to terrorism. As Jessie Daniels explains of the relationship between white feminism and statecraft, "white feminism functions like a war machine in that it wants to accomplish feminist goals in and through the State."[67] Bush's rhetoric directed attention to everyday aspects of biological life (e.g., the ability to go to school, make a living wage, participate in politics) and the extent to which the US intervention meant those aspects would no longer be subject to terrorist threats, rather than focusing on the effects of state violence and war. Establishing infrastructure for capitalism is key to liberal war, as

Dana L. Cloud summarizes with regard to the implied narrative for the War on Terror: "America plus capitalism equals democracy . . . anti-American plus pre-capitalism equals barbarity."[68] School creation for girls and women, transportation to schools, and access to knowledge become significant minutiae in the biopoliticization of civil society in Afghanistan.[69] At least since the Spanish-American and Philippine-American Wars (1898–1902), which were US interventions to civilize brown and Black peoples in developing countries, "liberalism," writes Evans, "declares otherness to be *the* problem to be solved."[70] Thus, amid criticisms about the failures of so-called smart war technologies, the War on Terror appeared to be humane and quieted calls for peace in the stories about the betterment of Afghan women.[71] The war was constructed as an opportunity for growth and change rather than destruction, a feminist venture with adversity rather than with violence, and a venture undertaken on behalf of Afghan women rather than an externally imposed reform.

By fighting sexism with racism, the white feminist invention of a gender divide distracts from colonial power structures and governmental politics, and in turn draws scrutiny to Afghan culture and Islamic fundamentalism as preventing the advancement of women.[72] With the feminist advocacy of the First Lady, the American military enterprise could be seen as a nonviolent and progressive resource for creating infrastructure, welcoming foreign investors and business, and opening up the country and culture to different values and external influences.[73] Through the U.S.-Afghan Women's Council, an organization for which Laura Bush is the honorary adviser, the First Lady campaigned for American public-private partnerships that would offer entrepreneurial support for Afghan women.[74] Her rhetoric on the War on Terror argued that if it was won, Afghanistan could become an economically flourishing country where its people, particularly women, could exercise democratic values and participate in capitalism. Bush stated the importance of globalizing feminism: "Our dedication to respecting and protecting women's rights in all countries must continue if we are to achieve a peaceful, prosperous, and stable world."[75] She described literacy as a means of producing colonial subjects that will support neoliberal policies. In order for women's rights to materialize, Afghan women need literacy to become good mothers for their children:

> Women in every society are the ones who make most of the choices for their children. They make the choices of what foods to serve; they many times make the health care choices for their children. And if they are educated, they are more likely to be able to make informed choices so that their

children don't suffer from malnutrition, so that their children can receive the best health care.[76]

Literacy is pursued not for education's sake, but for the purposes of establishing a competitive economy and of generating an improved biopolitical life for Afghan subjects who make good decisions.[77] As the First Lady asserted on the *Today* show: "If people are educated, economies are better. We know that the countries with the highest education rates also have the best economies."[78] Bush's feminist advocacy of literacy in Afghanistan aimed to establish a Western-influenced economy and citizenry and, ultimately, a wall against terrorism that would help protect global capitalism and Western interests. Maria Raha explains of white feminism's relationship with war, "Supporting the welfare of the world's women means supporting the war on terrorism—and, more insidious, supporting the war on terrorism means supporting the world's women, with no further action required."[79] Addressing the basic needs and desires of Afghan women through literacy, education, and infrastructure would bring forth a post–War on Terror state in Afghanistan—pro-democracy capitalist economy—that would be a more attractive alternative to al-Qaeda for Afghan citizens. Bush mobilized global motherhood not only through her own performativity but also through her rhetoric of liberal war's possibility in producing Afghan women as good mothers of and for their own communities.

Importantly, Western standards of feminine beauty and dress were part of Bush's feminist rhetoric as well. When Bush suggested that painting their nails would be dangerous under the Taliban regime in her 2001 radio address, she established common interests in beauty and humanized the burqa-wearing Afghan woman as desirous of the colonial gaze. Mimi Thi Nguyen astutely argues, "Against the burqa, the hair curler or the eyeliner emerges as a political referendum on the fundamentalist regime; the Afghan woman who desires beauty thus desires a democratic future of movement, choice, and independence, where beauty is imagined to live."[80] In this future democratic Afghanistan, Bush suggests that Afghan women can dress, think, and care for themselves freely. Minh-Ha Pham points out, "the fashion-as-a-right discourse . . . and the humanitarian rhetoric of the war on terror are mutually constitutive."[81] Thus, when Bush discussed the burqa as an oppressive style of dress that inhibits Afghan women from revealing their true identities, she constructs Afghan women as eager for and receptive to American intervention. After celebrating the Taliban's diminishing influence, Bush quoted an Afghan woman, Shura, as saying, "For five years, we could not recognize each other on the street because of our burqas. Now we can be together and try to fight."[82]

While the quotation insinuates that burqas inhibit political organizing and feminist expression, the most important implication of Bush's rhetoric is that the burqa is not a self-chosen style of dress and not constitutive of agency.[83] Meyda Yeğenoğlu explains the significance of white feminism in the process of westernizing the other: "There was a *simulation of sovereign masculine discourse* by Western women. It is in the East that Western woman was able to become a full individual, which was the goal desired and promoted by the emerging modernist ideology. Hence, for Western women it was possible to achieve the desired subject status against a devalued *cultural difference*."[84] This Western feminist construction of Afghan women as wanting to be unveiled not only implies a rhetorical sameness with white women but also suggests Afghan women's current invisibility in a sexist regime. To marshal feminist support for war, Bush projected feminine passivity and victimhood onto Afghan women who really want makeovers and perform Western practices of beauty. Treating agency as caught between the binaries of obedience and rebellion, compliance and resistance, and submission and subversion is a white feminist strategy that justifies the continuation of liberal war.[85]

Bush's global mother feminism successfully rallied bipartisan support for the War on Terror. The Feminist Majority Foundation lauded the First Lady as a lone champion of women's rights in Afghanistan.[86] Despite criticism about women and children being most victimized by NATO bombs and military violence, feminists agreed with Bush's global mother feminism and claimed that women and children's security and progress should be a condition on which peace is agreed.[87] Mariella Frostrup opines, "Basic recognition of women's human rights must be a qualifying requirement for peace."[88] In other words, the feminist position was that liberal war's benefits override the issues of morality and violence in military invasion and occupation.[89] However, Jennifer L. Fluri provides local nuance to the feminist argument, explaining that "efforts by former Kabul governments to 'modernize,' and liberate and/or improve women's educational and economic opportunities . . . throughout the twentieth century, were largely limited to women of higher socioeconomic classes, larger ethnic groups, and/or women living in Kabul."[90] Instead of a critical engagement about what it means to install democracy by force, what corporate stakes motivate American interests in Afghanistan, or even whether American military skill, technology, and prowess would best terrorist forces, feminism centered the conversation about invading Afghanistan on how American presence would enhance biopolitical protection of Afghan life along the sex binary. As Dillon and Reid explain of the emancipatory function of liberal war, "the more the emancipatory politics of the biohuman circumscribes the politics of emancipation, specifically in seeking to make war to remove the scourge of war from the human, the more intensively do biopolitical imperatives intrude into everyday life, and the more extensively are they applied globally."[91] The American debate between war as a biopolitical venture and war as a standard colonial endeavor was smoothed over with a third option: war that would uniquely benefit Afghan women, who are just as concerned as white women about their own biopolitical life.

First Lady Bush recast the war effort as a humanitarian undertaking to care for Afghan women who had simple interests in common with white women: wanting to provide for their families, to walk freely, to laugh out loud, to wear painted fingernails, and to be educated. Fixated on the gender of the subjects that would be saved, feminism inflected liberal war with global motherhood both as a figuration for its cause and as a performativity that would be had. As a liberal war waged on the grounds of securing the quality of biological life, the War on Terror privileged discussions about educational and business infrastructure or electricity or running water over discussions of morality and the violence of war. The purported postwar benefits put forward through global motherhood enabled feminism to accept colonial violence. A liberal war abroad in Afghanistan sharply contrasts with and deflects from necropolitical issues inside the United States and its military ally Canada, including limited access to clean water, food insecurity, and job discrimination—all issues that many Indigenous, Black, and racialized peoples experience.[92]

Conclusion

The figuration of the global mother as someone who cares for her own family and her community brought liberal and conservative feminisms together in support of First Lady Bush and Palin. While Palin may be mean and unstylized and Bush may be genial and composed, both Bush and Palin established political and moral leadership through global mother feminism. Whereas Bush's global motherhood registered as natural and expected of her role as First Lady, Palin's global motherhood was seen as polarizing, despite the long history of negative narrative in electoral politics. Their political advocacy and career trajectory resonate with Louise Michele Newman's insight on a previous era that "white women who carried out this civilization-work at home among Native Americans, the urban poor, and immigrants became a part of the ruling class of the progressive era without having to press their own claims for the elective franchise to obtain political power."[93]

As this chapter has shown, I question the grounds on which white feminists interpret opposition to white womanhood as sexist. Civilization discourse and work are not from a bygone era; they are essential to the contemporary production of white womanhood, allowing white women to "act as representatives to the primitive without violating notions of 'woman's sphere' or abrogating their conventional duties as wives and mothers."[94] Conservativism is treated by white feminists as an ideological orientation that deserves dialogical engagement rather than as a key contributor to the systems of power that underpin racial conflicts. Narrowing the differences between conservative and liberal politics, feminism strengthened embourgeoisement in politics that furthered racial resentment. In the cases of Bush and Palin, liberal feminism's defense of conservative feminism promoted the white capacity to determine care and quality of life as feminine and feminist. Hopefully, I have shown how global mother feminism crucially lacks a holistic approach. Koa Beck explains that a holistic approach

> addresses the reality of people's lives and that involves not only marginalized genders being seen, but securing food and basic resources like clean water and housing. Then workplace protections, decent wages, and a reformed justice system. Finally, once basic needs, workplace protections, and our legal system are secured, women and nonbinary people need the opportunities to grow through education and small-business opportunities. White feminism has never been this movement.[95]

Bush and Palin's white feminism has never been this movement. Global mother feminism gatekeeps sovereignty and expands white biopower by reconstructing colonial violence as an opportunity to extend care to the self, family, nation, and globe.

ABOLISHING MEAN
GIRL FEMINISM

"The personal is political" is a slogan that has inspired and guided feminist advocacy on a range of political issues, including intimate partner violence and marriage and divorce law. This mantra deconstructs the binary of private and public spheres that upholds traditional gender roles and heteronormative expectations. "The personal is political" has also been applied as a heuristic for understanding certain forms of performativity and expressions of womanhood as feminist. Because the feminine body moves in and through various spheres of life, political boundaries do not end in the public sphere, and feminism advocates for nuanced understanding of embodiment. However, as I have tried to show, that nuanced understanding from white feminism ends with gender. White feminism organizes an affective economy that circulates white women's aggression and microaggressions as performative reactions to cis-heteropatriarchy and feminine vulnerability. Not fitting into patriarchal notions of proper femininity, mean girl feminism produces the category of gender as if it were resistance itself, as if intention of gender performativity were a form of emancipation, as if women were free from power's effects and implications. This book has explored the various ways in which feminism puts forward and even celebrates white mean girls as the ideal figures of resistance. Performativity itself can be a spectacle of doing and acting in the world, and this book has tried to raise doubt about performativity as a means of feminist resistance.

Mean girl feminism emphasizes meanness as antipatriarchal expression and at the same time promotes white womanhood as the trappings of that feminist performativity. I have analyzed meanness and white womanhood together to take notice of the various ways in which the damsel in distress has transformed into the damsel in resistance, someone who gaslights, gatekeeps, and girlbosses in her performativity. Chapter 1 examined how feminism focuses on performativity as agency that either assimilates or resists patriarchal norms, a false binary that discourages discussion about intersectional feminist liberation and modes of dismantling imperialist white supremacist capitalist cis-heteropatriarchy. *The Bitch Manifesto* (1968), the notion of resting bitch face (RBF), and girlboss characters like Diana St. Tropez of *Great News* (2017–18) resignify Bitch as a white figure whose words and performative refusal to embrace traditional feminine comportment are important individual acts of patriarchal subversion. This boss Bitch or girlboss figure is driven by professional success and neoliberal values, and she is unwilling to be moved by romance or friendship. Her hardened shell and independence are a result of patriarchal exclusion, and now she is willing to be as ruthless as a white man, often by stealing strategies and tactics of racialized survival. What is a racist slur and figure of empowerment for Black women is here deracialized, transformed into a white feminist who responds to gendered oppression with wit, snark, sarcasm, humor, and other means of communication and performativity that are within women's control. Bitch feminism individualizes meanness's success into girlboss rubrics of intelligence and performativity.

Chapter 2 continues this line of inquiry about the performative turn with particular attention to how white feminism embeds antipatriarchal meaning in signifiers that are not traditionally feminine: wearing pants instead of skirts, posting room decor celebrating that the future is female, not putting on makeup, and engaging in other aspects of performativity that point attention to the body but are not inherent to it. Through an analysis of the movie *Mean Girls* (2004) and white feminist scholarship on the beauty myth and illegible rage, I discuss how the distinction between feminism and postfeminism is dependent on rebuking and exposing hyperfemininity as antifeminist. In mean girl feminism, because the beautiful girl is mean—and because she bathes in the glow of the male gaze and its rewards of popularity and wealth—she must be exposed. However, both the mean girl and the damsel in resistance exemplify exceptionalist inclusion into cis-heteropatriarchy. Through confrontations with girls and women who are winning the white heteronormative male gaze, feminism constructs itself as the moral advocate of pure gender analysis, unfettered by race or other identity differences. While postfeminism is seen as problematically individualizing feminist action into neoliberal advancement and embourgeoisement, feminism too individualizes feminist action, rendering it as intentional, performative signifiers of and on the body that deviate from traditional gender roles and femininity. White feminism aims to come out on top as the good guy by recognizing the faults of postfeminism or neoliberal feminism as other than its own. By arguing that postfeminism, neoliberal feminism, and other forms of feminism are not feminist enough, white gender studies embraces meanness as a tool for feminist gatekeeping in order to mark out what is and is not feminist.

Also part of the affective economy of white feminism's mean girl empire are the ways in which monogamous heteronormativity furthers white feminine interiority and virtue. As considered in chapter 3, the power couple trope accentuates work-life balance as an important pivot to putting popular feminism in practice. Love helps construct heterosociality as structured not by feminist envy of the ideal subject position of the white heterosexual male but by the competing demands of economic and affective planes that need to be negotiated. With work-life balance as a core tension complicating feminism's amenability to patriarchal power structures, the mean girl figure of the power couple renders monogamous romantic love as compatible with the white male-female binary of acceptable aggression: his sexual prowess and her managerial skill. The queen bee's harsh love can tame the sexual predations of white toxic masculinity, which in turn is redeemed and can be resourced for feminist means and ends. The mean girl feminist shows that while she may not be able to quell or organize a catty girl squad, she can work with difference and use the strategies and feelings of building community toward making her own coupledom and family. Her willingness to love violent men is a form of gaslighting, rendering imperialist white supremacist capitalist cis-heteropatriarchy nonviolent.

In chapter 4, global motherhood contributes to the drama of the white mean girl empire as it is mobilized to civilize racialized women for the biological advancement of society. I take to heart Rafia Zakaria's insight that "carrying forward the racial hierarchies and self-interested exploitation of the colonial era, white feminists have identified progress not as renouncing wars and empire but as competing with white men at the tasks of neo-imperialism."[1] Both First Lady Laura Bush and vice presidential candidate Sarah Palin reanimate the ideology of global motherhood as a biopolitical technology that safeguards white customs and ways of life. With the added defense of liberal feminists protective of the gender binary, Bush and Palin tether feminism to statecraft in ways that expand white biopower into the domain of gender performativity.

Mean girl feminism advocates for a politics of performativity that promotes equity between white people. If whiteness as a phenomenology readies the world for certain bodies, then mean girl feminism readies the world for white women and their diverse, unstereotypical approaches to bodily comportment and performativity.[2] What I have tried to show throughout this book is how the harms of feminism are inscribed in the performative turn to meanness, which isolates white womanhood as the mode of agency, mobility, and power. The performative turn in feminism focuses on presenting oneself as feminist, rather than on enacting and living feminism. In so doing, feminism distances itself from hyperfemininity and feminism's fringe movements, casting them as sign(ifier)s of antifeminism. This rhetorical distancing sets the stage for feminism to moralize and cling harder to gender analysis as an escape that fails to confront the violence of imperialist white supremacist capitalist cis-heteropatriarchy.

While a politics of recognition has its faults, I know that recognition is a sustaining and life-affirming desire for all subjects, and feminism's subjects are no different in wanting to resist invisibility. Feminism has received greater visibility through performativity that roughens imperialist white supremacist capitalist cis-heteropatriarchy with meanness and bitchiness. However, by creating an abrasive white femininity within the scope of feminism, mean girl feminism reinvents and updates femininity as a coping strategy for the harsh conditions of the status quo. Meanness both acknowledges the pain of the cruel optimism of contemporary power structures that gradually evolve, make progress, and widen its range of recognition, and at the same time refuses to devolve into anger.

Over the course of this book, I have argued that in a milieu in which feminism is being called on to become more aware of race, white feminism has co-opted the very meanness that has been used to draw attention to racism, using it to dig harder into gender analysis. The advancement of a pure gender analysis becomes the means and the ends of feminism. As a kind of negativity that does not name power and oppression, meanness redirects collective energy onto the individual white woman who needs to get her way. As Lauren Berlant explains in *The Female Complaint*: "What was a minor register of survival aesthetics has also become a predominant way even for elites to orchestrate a claim that their social discomfort amounts to evidence of injustice to them."[3] White women make meanness part of the politics of their recognition, and in effect, racialized meanness is seen as uncontrollable, not consumable, dangerous.

Acknowledging feminism's fractured history, Kyla Schuller argues that feminism's imperfections are precisely what makes feminism an important topos: "Feminists may support equality for women, but our true task is to determine what exactly equality looks like. The feminist movement is the grounds of an ongoing struggle to hash out the theories, methods, and goals that might bring us closer to gender, racial, and economic justice. . . . But the history of feminism is the history of the fight to define feminism, to determine what it advocates and whom it represents. This internal tension doesn't compromise feminism—it comprises it."[4] The internal tension within feminism comprises struggle against oppression and injustice. If intersectionality is a kind of ethic and ethical frame by which feminism should abide, then the collective solidarity that is constitutive of feminist ends is also a constant struggle to articulate them with subaltern counterparts. This is what I believe gets lost when good-intentioned folks strive for the best life and better circumstances. As Sara Ahmed puts it, for "paper feminists"—those who are feminist on paper but not in practice—white liberal feminism can be about "how a white woman's career advancement is made dependent on keeping her distance from complaints and complainers."[5]

Racialized Mean Girls

It is unlikely that the mean girl figuration will be laid to rest anytime soon, as it has grown to be a popular source to imagine and engage the performativity of feminism within imperialist white supremacist capitalist cis-heteropatriarchy. This is especially problematic when women of color perform meanness, to which I'd like to turn because there are substantive differences in the racialized performativity of meanness in popular culture. The movies *Little* (2019) and *What Men Want* (2019) both star Black women as mean girls having to reckon with male-dominated corporate culture. Meanness is constructed as a product of neoliberal feminism and Black vernacular neoliberalism, the latter being a "substantial political shift in which selfishness and privatisation have displaced racial structures onto an interpersonal scale and facilitated the replacement of imperfect democracy by what we are told is the non-negotiable force of a natural hierarchy."[6] While Jordan Sanders (Regina Hall) in *Little* resorts to meanness as a result of early traumatic experiences with racism, and Ali Davis (Taraji P. Henson) in *What Men Want* becomes mean from continual discrimination while working at a sports agency, Sanders and Davis adopt the same coping method: maximizing neoliberal opportunity and subjecting others to the harsh conditions and values of the capitalist work ethic and achievement.

However, the meanness of these Black women protagonists acknowledges the intersection of racism and cis-heteropatriarchy, and, as a result, these movies end differently than those texts analyzed in my earlier chapters. By showing Jordan's childhood and Ali's repeated discrimination, the movies illustrate that their meanness emerges out of lived experience, and there is a historical reason for their hostility. Unlike in *Mean Girls* and *Crash* (2004), where the happy ending is made possible through near-fatal injuries inflicted on white mean girls (and the reorganization of cliques along common interests), Jordan and Ali make amends with the characters they have mistreated. Unlike in *Desperate Housewives* (2004–12) and *Little Fires Everywhere* (2020), where the characters see the effects of their behaviors but do not take responsibility, Black women characters become aware of the harm of their meanness and gesture toward accountability. Racialized meanness emerges with a different, intersectional relationship to power structures and emerges with a different futurity, one that is oriented toward justice, even in the style and constraints of Hollywood.

But meanness is a fragile dance that is already familiar to racialized actors. Gabrielle Union describes it well in her memoir, aptly titled *You Got Anything Stronger?* (2021). Union costarred in the movie *Bring It On* (2000), where a white cheer team, led by Torrance (Kirsten Dunst), steals the routines of a Black cheer squad of which Union plays the captain, Isis. Writing directly to her character but with two decades of hindsight, Union reflects on the production process and the way that she made her character "more authentically Black" by finessing the script to address cultural appropriation. But, speaking of one key scene in which Isis and her teammates confront Torrance for recording their routines and then Isis allows Torrance to simply leave, without physical escalation, Union reveals, speaking to Isis: "I thought you had to give [white people] grace in the face of thievery. You had every right to ask them to come forward publicly about what they had done, seek forgiveness, and work toward justice. But I made you educate, yet again, people who absolutely know better and still refuse to do better." With regret, Union wishes she had "not muzzle[d] any of that rage, including the justifiable anger" of her character's teammates.[7] Union's reflection about Black woman embodiment and performativity suggests that meanness would have meant holding Torrance and the white cheer team accountable.

In this brief engagement of racialized meanness, some differences should become apparent from what I have illustrated so far in this book. While meanness is a familiar coping strategy for people of color, meanness is not a manifesto for a feminist future, as *The Bitch Manifesto* is for white feminism. Meanness is not an inarticulate drive of feminist invisibility and underutilized talent, as it is for a white feminist politics. Meanness is not a tool for managing white male violence for domestic bliss and redemption, as it is for the power couples of white feminism. Meanness is not a means of validating the racial superiority of white motherhood, as it is for the global mothers of white feminism.

As an effect of being positioned as subaltern, racially marginalized people use meanness when their agency to be, to say, to do has been taken, co-opted, appropriated, and silenced. Rather, meanness can facilitate a world in which racialized people can draw attention to the harms they face and the pain caused by those harms. As Enrique Alemán Jr. has argued, "the politics of building coalitions and establishing allies amid an atmosphere of niceness prohibits blatant and honest depictions of racialized oppression."[8] Being inarticulate, not having enough evidence, not knowing the logic of the best argument all are part of the problem of being subaltern. These ideas are well explored by Ahmed's complaint feminism and the figure of the feminist killjoy, which describe how marginalized people complain about and call attention to the uncomfortable truths of oppression. These ideas are also discussed in Patricia Hill Collins's figuration of Bitches who support their communities.[9] Both intersectional figurations cannot be detached from their racialized context as their resistant quality of meanness engages the materiality of various oppressions. They cannot be separated from the subaltern relationships that are necessary for anti-oppressive work and research.[10] Furthermore, both forms of meanness are not about defending an expansive notion of performance for individuals but about supporting collective action and liberation. As Ahmed rightly worries about the feminist killjoy, "A killjoy becomes a manifesto when we are willing to take up this figure, to assemble a life *not as her but around her, in her company*."[11] Being a killjoy and being a Bitch is not about *you* being a killjoy or being a Bitch: it is about *her*. The killjoy and the Bitch make space for one's community because meanness is not enough, and its effects should be connected to collective struggle with the subaltern.

Neither gender nor race alone can function as a form of self-affirmation. Following the scholarship of Frantz Fanon, Glen Coulthard argues that cultural self-affirmation "constituted an important 'means' but 'not an ultimate end' of anticolonial struggle."[12] Meanness may help challenge or call attention to structural oppression, but, as already suggested, it does not operate as an endpoint for decolonial feminism as it does for white feminism. If it did, meanness as a practice would risk serving as "a source of pride and empowerment" that could "easily become a cluster of antiquated attachments that divert attention away from the present and future needs" of the colonized.[13] Ruby Hamad affirms the lack of materiality in performative politics: "To separate identity from economics and land rights and language turns culture into little more than those exhibitions found at arts festivals and multicultural events, a spectacle that exists for others to enjoy and consume."[14] The turn to feminist performativity neglects the ways in which white women may be killjoys or bitches only on weekdays, only in (work)spaces of potential capitalist accumulation, only at times when confronted by the effects of colonial oppression, only when a prettier person steals the white masculine gaze, and only to signal that gender difference is at play.

The inconsistency around white feminist performativity can be seen in the many tweets and social media posts of surprise or new frustration that progressive white women have in reaction to their family's opposition to Black Lives Matter, as if that is the first time they have spoken about race with their family members. The inconsistency around white feminist performativity can be seen in the white feminist cheeky calls to "save Melania (Trump)" by women married to someone who voted for Donald Trump, as evidenced in photos of competing his and hers lawn signs (him voting for Trump, her voting for Hillary Clinton). The inconsistency around white feminist performativity can be seen in the performed lamentations and outreach to women of color, maneuvers that ignore "how Black bodies have historically been your solace in a myriad of ways."[15] The inconsistency around white feminist performativity can be seen in how J. K. Rowling uses the sex binary to show that she is oppressed rather than how the sex binary itself is oppressive, to trans folks included. The inconsistency around feminist performativity can be seen in the commitments by white feminist celebrities to denounce racism, which is on trend after Darnella Frazier's widely disseminated recording of Minneapolis police officers murdering George Floyd in 2020. If the personal is political, then why were white feminist women only just now engaging in political discussions at the dinner table? How long and how deep will white women care about racism as Floyd's tragic death recedes into history? Attending a protest or speaking publicly about an issue requires a register or praxis that is different from what one uses to critically engage the microaggressions among family or engage in frank discussions with friends about their flakiness or inconsistent practice of care. Are white women ready and willing to face social death for making the personal political?

One way of challenging white womanhood both in terms of performativity and on its own terms would be to look back at Jessie Daniel Ames and the Association of Southern Women for the Prevention of Lynching (ASWPL), founded in 1930. They sought to "strike down the apologetics of lynching by disassociating the image of the lady from its connotations of female vulnerability and retaliatory violence." Ames's advocacy aimed to question "the crown of chivalry which has been pressed like a crown of thorns on our heads."[16] In order to show how white womanhood helped solidify racial and gender lines of civility, Ames's leadership in the anti-lynching movement was motivated by the argument that only 29 percent of the 204 Black men victimized by lynching in 1922–30 were accused of crimes against white women. The white women of the ASWPL recognized their own performativity in exemplifying the norms of ladyhood on which lynching was reliant, as a means of constructing and performing "their own definition of responsible womanhood."[17] I turn to Ames as an example because redefining "responsible womanhood" involved talking openly about how their own performativity and identity construction were constitutive of their feminism. Feminism must "refuse the racist definitions of white femininity."[18] Abolishing mean girl feminism means refusing the virtue that imbues feminist resistance with a nonviolent and progressive valence. The choice is not about women being submissive or resistant to gender norms; rather, white feminists need to recognize the violent effects of the white performative body, even when the body might be responding to sexism.

Where traditional femininity might emphasize innocence and niceness, mean girl feminism encourages women to interpret Collins's figure of the Bitch and Ahmed's figure of the feminist killjoy as if they were an identity category to be performed, a personhood that has assumed permanence—a defiant attitude, the unsmiling face. If mean girl feminism is about performance and performativity, then it inevitably leaves some women and others behind: women who do not act feminist and bitchy, those who act "too" feminine or femme, nonbinary folks whose performativity might not support a feminism based on the category of women. Often, the white women who articulate their quick wits well in the workplace are now the administrators who espouse diversity; the white women who challenge gender roles at home are now the employers of "the help" and racialized labor. Collective action and sustained dismantling of violent systems are not part of the conversation in mean girl feminism.

To not conflate willfulness and individualism, Ahmed issues an invitation: "To make manifesto out of the killjoy means being willing to give to others the support you received or wish you received. . . . Don't let her speak on her own. Back her up; speak with her. Stand by her; stand with her. From these public moments of solidarity so much is brought into existence. We are creating a support system around the killjoy; we are finding ways to allow her to do what she does, to be who she is."[19] It is not about you or me; it is about *her/them*.

Instead of the girlboss figure, who individualizes leadership on display, decolonial feminism would share the stage, not just the work and labor. Recently, I attended a workshop on mentoring equity work to take back to our institutional settings. Throughout the presentation, the facilitator, a white woman, cited the work of many racialized authors about the importance of building community and relationships to help shield and shelter vulnerable peoples amid the violence of institutions. She did an excellent job speaking woke, talking about radical care, writing a thoughtful land acknowledgment, listening to our contributions after a group activity. Telling us to build relationships and helping us identify ways in which care can be extended sure did feel like decolonial feminist work. But decolonial feminism was not embodied in the workshop model, which felt extractive and performative. I had attended two other workshops with similar content, but those were led or co-led by racialized leaders and organizers. Furthermore, they were created in response to international traumatic events, not envisioned as methods to support the upkeep of institutional power. Why didn't the white feminist bring in a racialized scholar to co-lead (instead of maintaining a distance from racialized people through citation and lecture), share this opportunity both monetarily and professionally, and model how to build and mentor a relationship and community in the very work of working on equity? For some white feminists, a progressive model of co-leadership involves the power couple, where the romantic partner also becomes the business partner; or the racialized graduate student or junior faculty member who is not on equal terms. Koa Beck reminds us that "the revolution will not be you alone, despite what white feminism has told you. There is only the resistant movements that you will build with other people."[20]

Finally, feminism also needs to rethink its relationship with men/masculinity. The feminists of Development Alternatives with Women for a New Era, who developed the empowerment approach in South Asia, argued that equality with men could not be their guiding principle since men "themselves suffered employment, low wages, poor work conditions and racism within existing socio-economic structures."[21] This particular kind of feminism that is women led is not the same as white feminism because the goal is to free everyone, not just themselves. Being a Vietnamese refugee, speaking little English, living on public assistance, taking care of four children and a working wife, my dad learned of the public hatred directed toward the groups to which he belonged. My dad's response, not being formally educated, was to identify with that conservative resentment. When I became eligible to vote, I wanted to learn about my dad's political leanings. It was through my consistent discussion with him that we agreed that this public hatred was a problem and decided to vote otherwise. As someone who was going to pursue education as an occupation, I found it vital to have his support, and I am glad to say that my dad became part of my decolonial feminist future as much as I have worked to value his. I draw on this example because it would be typical of a white feminist reading to dwell on the gender difference between my dad and me in my retelling of our interaction. While that definitely played a part in our conversations, dwelling on that component in my retelling would reinscribe my own virtue and make me more innocent than him. *Listen to this sexist comment he said.* It would allow me to position my dad as a patriarchal villain to feminism and to position myself as more moral and feminist. Furthermore, this would contribute to the performance of Oppression Olympics, which discourage finding solidarity and building community for the sake of identifying the worst victim. Feminist resistance, especially at the intersection, is violent and uncomfortable, and we should be careful about ascribing innocence or virtue to feminist advocacy.

If, as bell hooks urges, feminism is a "struggle"—rather than "a lifestyle [or] a ready-made identity or role"—then naming power's strategies and the people and subject positions that may be performing those strategies is part of the feminist struggle.[22] Naming mean girl feminism has been a performative contradiction. I have tried to "write into our contradiction" so that the next step is to hold ourselves accountable to the subaltern and the vernaculars and dialects they speak and understand.[23] This is essential if feminism aims to move beyond entrepreneurial politics or power couples or mean girl cliques, whose dynamics mobilize sameness and maintain systems of power. These dynamics absolve those with power and privilege and fail to deconstruct the ways in which dominant ideologies create the subaltern in the first place.

Considering how racialized anger can be co-opted and appropriated, solidarity with *her/them* means recognizing that the subaltern may not appear, so we must wait. Solidarity with *her/them* means recognizing that the subaltern may not speak, so we must listen. Solidarity with *her/them* means recognizing that the subaltern might not be alone, so we must widen our scope. Feminism in the future—a decolonial feminism—might not be recognizable as a feminism at all.

Notes

Preface

1. I want to recognize that Kimberly Foster uses the phrase "mean girl feminism" in a YouTube video; see Kimberly Foster, "I'm Done with Mean Girl Feminism (an Ayesha Curry Rant)," YouTube video, posted May 9, 2019, by For Harriet, 20:13, https://www.youtube.com/watch?v=byybf63-eTI. I thank Jade Jacobs (@JadeSJacobs) for bringing this to my attention.

2. Rafia Zakaria, *Against White Feminism: Notes on Disruption* (New York: W.W. Norton, 2021), 202.

3. Koa Beck, *White Feminism: From Suffragettes to Influencers and Who They Leave Behind* (London: Simon and Schuster, 2021), xvii.

4. Carol Anderson, *White Rage: The Unspoken Truth of Our Racial Divide* (New York: Bloomsbury, 2016), 3.

5. Kimberlé Crenshaw, "Demarginalizing the Intersection of Race and Sex: A Black Feminist Critique of Antidiscrimination Doctrine, Feminist Theory and Antiracist Politics," *University of Chicago Legal Forum* 1 (1989): 139–67.

6. Zakaria, *Against White Feminism*, 51.

7. It is important to note that Melania Trump delivered a speech at the 2016 Republican National Convention that plagiarized Michelle Obama's 2008 Democratic National Convention speech. See "US Election: Melania Trump 'Plagiarised' Michelle Obama," BBC News, July 19, 2016.

8. Kelsey Weekman, "Gen Z Is Poking Fun at Both Moms and Manipulators with a Catchy, Three-Word Mantra," *Yahoo News*, May 4, 2021, https://news.yahoo.com/.

9. Alex Abad-Santos, "The Death of the Girlboss," *Vox*, June 7, 2021, https://www.vox.com/22466574/gaslight-gatekeep-girlboss-meaning.

10. Craig Fortier discusses the risk of non-Indigenous responsibility to decolonization and ways in which they have tried to address it through their research. See Fortier,

"Unsettling Methodologies/Decolonizing Movements," *Journal of Indigenous Social Development* 6 (2017): 20–36.

11. While non-white characters may be featured, the texts discussed in this book primarily originate from or occur in North America, and therefore I analyze them as being governed by whiteness. See Thomas Nakayama and Robert Krizek, "Whiteness: A Strategic Rhetoric," *Quarterly Journal of Speech* 81 (1995): 291–309.

12. I borrow the term *popular feminism* from Sarah Banet-Weiser, who coined it to refer to a commodified form of white feminism that claims to empower women but only according to the accumulative logics of neoliberalism; see Banet-Weiser, *Empowered: Popular Feminism and Popular Misogyny* (Durham, NC: Duke University Press, 2018).

13. Lauren Berlant, *The Female Complaint: The Unfinished Business of Sentimentality in American Culture* (Durham, NC: Duke University Press, 2008), 4, 5.

14. I borrow the term *imperialist white supremacist capitalist cis-heteropatriarchy* from bell hooks, who modified her original formulation to describe the systemic oppression that governs our world. See Laverne Cox and bell hooks, "bell hooks: a conversation with Laverne Cox," *Appalachian Heritage* 43 (2015): 24–40.

15. Nigel Thrift, *Non-Representational Theory: Space, Politics, Affect* (London: Routledge, 2007), 19.

16. Beck, *White Feminism*, 83.

17. Sara Ahmed, *Living a Feminist Life* (Durham, NC: Duke University Press, 2017), 255 (emphasis added).

18. Beck, *White Feminism*, xvii.

19. Beck, xviii.

Introduction. Feminist Civility and the Right to Be Mean

1. For the music video, see "Taylor Swift- Mean," YouTube video, posted May 13, 2011, by Taylor Swift, 4:03, https://www.youtube.com/watch?v=jYa1eI1hpDE.

2. For a brief consideration of Swift's use of girl power as feminist, see Camille Paglia, "Camille Paglia Takes on Taylor Swift, Hollywood's #GirlSquad Culture," *Hollywood Reporter*, December 10, 2015.

3. I use the term *girl* in accordance with the way Marina Gonick theorizes "girl power" culture in neoliberalism, which represents girls as "the idealized forms of the self-determining individual" to contrast with the lack of self-esteem, voicelessness, and fragility of girls in their early psychological development. Gonick suggests that anxiety about white middle-class girlhood and proper womanhood is directed at adolescent girls as well as adult women. Marina Gonick, "Between 'Girl Power' and 'Reviving Ophelia': Constituting the Neoliberal Girl Subject," *NWSA Journal* 18, no. 2 (2006): 1–23. See also Jessica Ringrose, "A New Universal Mean Girl: Examining the Discursive Construction and Social Regulation of a New Feminine Pathology," *Feminism & Psychology* 16, no. 4 (2006): 405–24; Deirdre M. Kelly and Shauna Pomerantz, "Mean, Wild, and Alienated: Girls and the State of Feminism in Popular

Culture," *Girlhood Studies* 2, no. 1 (2009): 1–19. At the same time, I recognize that niceness is also prescribed for the performance of proper womanhood, as studied by Laurie A. Rudman and Peter Glick, "Prescriptive Gender Stereotypes and Backlash toward Agentic Women," *Journal of Social Issues* 57, no. 4 (2001): 743–62.

4. Koa Beck, *White Feminism: From Suffragettes to Influencers and Who They Leave Behind* (London: Simon and Schuster, 2021), 178.

5. I use the term *white womanhood* following Ruby Hamad and many other scholars analyzing womanhood as an exclusionary concept that is designed to identify "who counts as a woman." Hamad explains, "It's not about femininity and masculinity and how one should behave to be sufficiently one or the other, but about who counts as a woman and who counts as a man. Who counts as a human." Ruby Hamad, *White Tears/Brown Scars: How White Feminism Betrays Women of Color* (New York: Catapult, 2020), 124. While this work aims to counter that exclusion, I also follow Sara Ahmed's definition of feminism as "supporting women in a struggle to exist in this world," which means supporting "all those who travel under the sign *women*." Sara Ahmed, *Living a Feminist Life* (Durham, NC: Duke University Press, 2017), 14.

6. Vinay Menon, "Mainstreaming of Mean: Our Age of Nastiness, Deceit, and Malice," *Toronto Star*, November 15, 2013.

7. Melissa Gregg, "On Friday Night Drinks: Workplace Affects in the Age of the Cubicle," in *The Affect Theory Reader*, ed. Melissa Gregg and Gregory J. Seigworth (Durham, NC: Duke University Press, 2009), 250–68.

8. Soraya Roberts, "'Mean' People Top Forbes' List of Top-Earning Media Personalities," *Yahoo News*, November 4, 2014, https://news.yahoo.com/.

9. Gerald A. Voorhees, "Neoliberal Multiculturalism in Mass Effect: The Government of Difference in Digital Role-Playing Games," in *Dungeons, Dragons, and Digital Denizens: The Digital Role-Playing Game*, ed. Gerald A. Voorhees, Joshua Call, and Katie Whitlock (New York: Continuum International, 2012), 259–77.

10. Ann Laura Stoler, *Race and the Education of Desire: Foucault's History of Sexuality and the Colonial Order of Things* (Durham, NC: Duke University Press, 1995), 36–37.

11. See Gabrielle Moss, "Teen Mean Fighting Machine: Why Does the Media Love Mean Girls?," in *BITCHfest: Ten Years of Cultural Criticism from the Pages of Bitch Magazine*, ed. Lisa Jervis and Andi Zeisler (New York: Farrar, Straus, and Giroux, 2006), 43–48.

12. Hélène Cixous, "The Laugh of the Medusa," *Signs* 1, no. 4 (1976): 875–93.

13. Sheryl Sandberg, *Lean In: Women, Work, and the Will to Lead* (New York: Alfred Knopf, 2013); and see Beck, *White Feminism*, 193.

14. Sally Kohn, "Affirmative Action Has Helped White Women More Than Anyone," *TIME*, June 17, 2013.

15. I borrow the term *white prestige* from Stoler, who uses it to denote white privilege of subjects who are or seek to become bourgeois. At times, I use it interchangeably with white privilege.

16. Beck, *White Feminism*, 215.

17. Robyn Wiegman, *American Anatomies: Theorizing Race and Gender* (Durham, NC: Duke University Press, 1995), 117.

18. Hamad, *White Tears/Brown Scars*, 130–32.

19. Rebecca Traister, *Big Girls Don't Cry: The Election That Changed Everything for America* (New York: Free Press, 2010), 272.

20. Ahmed, *Living a Feminist Life*, 160, 174.

21. Alexander Weheliye, *Habeas Viscus: Racializing Assemblages, Biopolitics, and Black Feminist Theories of the Human* (Durham, NC: Duke University Press, 2014), 126.

22. Ahmed, *Living a Feminist Life*, 203.

23. Jay Dolmage, *Academic Ableism: Disability and Higher Education* (Ann Arbor: University of Michigan Press, 2017).

24. Sara Ahmed, *The Cultural Politics of Emotion* (Edinburgh: Edinburgh University Press, 2014), 35.

25. Jessie Daniels, *Nice White Ladies: The Truth about White Supremacy, Our Role in It, and How We Can Help to Dismantle It* (New York: Seal Press, 2021), 50.

26. Hamad, *White Tears/Brown Scars*, 101.

27. Sara Ahmed, "The Nonperformativity of Antiracism," *Meridians* 7, no. 1 (2006): 105. See also Michelle Daigle, "The Spectacle of Reconciliation: On (the) Unsettling Responsibilities to Indigenous Peoples in the Academy," *Environment and Planning D: Society and Space* 37, no. 4 (2019): 703–21.

28. For me, the performative turn is not same as the embodied turn in feminist politics, though they are related. For a discussion of embodied politics as performativity, see Natalie Fixmer and Julia Wood, "The Personal Is *Still* Political: Embodied Politics in Third Wave Feminism," *Women's Studies in Communication* 28, no. 2 (2005): 235–57.

29. Daniels, *Nice White Ladies*, 8.

30. See, respectively, Laura Kipnis, "(Male) Desire and (Female) Disgust: Reading Hustler," in *Cultural Studies*, ed. Lawrence Grossberg, Cary Nelson, and Paula Treichler (New York: Routledge, 1992), 373–91; Wendy Brown, *States of Injury: Power and Freedom in Late Modernity* (Princeton, NJ: Princeton University Press, 1995); Louise Michele Newman, *White Women's Rights: The Racial Origins of Feminism in the United States* (New York: Oxford University Press, 1999); Kyla Schuller, *The Trouble with White Women: A Counterhistory of Feminism* (New York: Bold Type Books, 2021); Jack Halberstam, "You Are Triggering Me! The Neo-Liberal Rhetoric of Harm, Danger and Trauma," *Bully Bloggers* (blog), July 5, 2014, https://bullybloggers.wordpress.com/2014/07/05/.

31. Mamta Motwani Accapadi, "When White Women Cry: How White Women's Tears Oppress Women of Color," *College Student Affairs Journal* 26, no. 2 (2007): 210.

32. Ann Laura Stoler, "Carnal Knowledge and Imperial Power: Gender, Race, and Morality in Colonial Asia," in *The Gender/Sexuality Reader: Culture, History, Political Economy*, ed. Roger N. Lancaster and Micaela di Leonardo (New York: Routledge, 1997), 19.

33. Stephanie Jones-Rogers, *They Were Her Property: White Women as Slave Owners in the American South* (New Haven, CT: Yale University Press, 2019).

34. Wendy Anderson, *Rebirthing a Nation: White Women, Identity Politics, and the Internet* (Jackson: University Press of Mississippi, 2021), 12.

35. Shawn Michelle Smith, *American Archives: Gender, Race, and Class in Visual Culture* (Princeton, NJ: Princeton University Press, 1999), 124.

36. Elizabeth Gillespie McRae, *Mothers of Massive Resistance: White Women and the Politics of White Supremacy* (New York: Oxford University Press, 2018), 3.

37. Hamad, *White Tears/Brown Scars*, 14.

38. Schuller, *The Trouble with White Women*, 4.

39. Laura Kipnis, *The Female Thing: Dirt, Sex, Envy, Vulnerability* (New York: Pantheon Books, 2006), 5 (qtd.), 7.

40. Beck, *White Feminism*, 118.

41. Newman, *White Women's Rights*.

42. Beck, *White Feminism*, 29.

43. Angela Davis, *Women, Race, & Class* (New York: Vintage Books, 1983); Barbara Ehrenreich, "Maid to Order," in *Rhetorical Visions: Reading and Writing in a Visual Culture*, ed. Wendy S. Hesford and Brenda Jo Brueggemann (Upper Saddle River, NJ: Pearson, 2007), 427–38.

44. Therese Saliba, "Military Presences and Absences: Arab Women and the Persian Gulf War," in *Seeing through the Media: The Persian Gulf War*, ed. Susan Jeffords and Lauren Rabinovitz (New Brunswick, NJ: Rutgers University Press, 1994), 263–84.

45. Robin DiAngelo, *White Fragility: Why It's So Hard for White People to Talk about Racism* (Boston: Beacon Press, 2018), 137.

46. Vron Ware, *Beyond the Pale: White Women, Racism, and History* (London: Verso, 1992), 37.

47. See Stoler, "Carnal Knowledge and Imperial Power."

48. Penelope Edmonds, "Unpacking Settler Colonialism's Urban Strategies: Indigenous Peoples in Victoria, British Columbia, and the Transition to a Settler-Colonial City," *Urban History Review* 38, no. 2 (2010): 12.

49. Ann Laura Stoler and Frederick Cooper, *Tensions of Empire: Colonial Cultures in a Bourgeois World* (Berkeley: University of California Press, 1997), 31.

50. For how space can be coded as white, see Setha Low, "Maintaining Whiteness: The Fear of Others and Niceness," *Transforming Anthropology* 17, no. 2 (2009): 79–92; Robin DiAngelo, "White Fragility," *International Journal of Critical Pedagogy* 3, no. 3 (2011): 54–70.

51. Cecily Jones, "Contesting the Boundaries of Gender, Race, and Sexuality in Barbadian Plantation Society," *Women's History Review* 12, no. 2 (2003): 224.

52. Schuller, *The Trouble with White Women*, 8.

53. See, respectively, Erin Rand, *Reclaiming Queer: Activist and Academic Rhetorics of Resistance* (Tuscaloosa: University of Alabama Press, 2014); Sara Ahmed, *The Promise of Happiness* (Durham, NC: Duke University Press, 2010); Sianne Ngai, *Ugly Feelings* (Cambridge, MA: Harvard University Press, 2007).

54. Giorgio Agamben, *Homo Sacer: Sovereign Power and Bare Life* (Stanford, CA: Stanford University Press, 1998), 174, 52. The possibility of a realm of unlawfulness, and the way the law's underside depends on the production of nonlegal states of exception, is disavowed in Agamben's work, as Alexander Weheliye makes so eloquently plain; see Weheliye, *Habeas Viscus*.

55. Benet Davetian, *Civility: A Cultural History* (Toronto: University of Toronto Press, 2009), 29.

56. Davetian, 355. For Davetian, rudeness is a category of civility that can be used to resist the performance of status and power, or to resist discursive conventions that constrain discussion about inequality.

57. Tavia Nyong'o and Kyla Wazana Tompkins, "Eleven Theses on Civility," *Social Text* (website), July 11, 2018, https://socialtextjournal.org/.

58. Schuller, *The Trouble with White Women*, 9.

59. Ahmed, *The Cultural Politics of Emotion*, 32.

60. Daniels, *Nice White Ladies*, 47. Daniels illustrates how white women's innocence and vulnerability puts up a facade of niceness that can turn dangerous for racialized people. When white women withhold meanness, they show how well the regime operates for themselves and for others.

61. Lauren Berlant, *The Female Complaint: The Unfinished Business of Sentimentality in American Culture* (Durham, NC: Duke University Press, 2008), 69.

62. See Ronald Walter Greene, "Rhetoric and Capitalism: Rhetorical Agency as Communicative Labor," *Philosophy and Rhetoric* 37 (2004): 188–206; Toby Miller, *The Well-Tempered Self: Citizenship, Culture, and the Postmodern Subject* (Baltimore, MD: Johns Hopkins University Press, 1991).

63. Weheliye, *Habeas Viscus*, 3.

64. Wiegman, *American Anatomies*, 97; see also Jessie Daniels, *White Lies: Race, Class, Gender, and Sexuality in White Supremacist Discourse* (New York: Routledge, 1997), 64; Jacquelyn Dowd Hall, *Revolt against Chivalry: Jessie Daniel Ames and the Women's Campaign against Lynching* (New York: Columbia University Press, 1979). On *The Birth of a Nation*, bell hooks explains, "Politics of race and gender were inscribed into mainstream cinematic narrative from *Birth of a Nation*. As a seminal work, this film identified what the place and function of white womanhood would be in cinema." bell hooks, "The Oppositional Gaze," in *Black Looks: Race and Representation*, by bell hooks (Boston: South End Press, 1992), 119–20.

65. DiAngelo, "White Fragility," 132.

66. Beverly Tatum notes, "62% of white women without college degrees voted for Trump, as did 45% of white women with college degrees." Beverly Tatum, *Why Are All the Black Kids Sitting Together in the Cafeteria? And Other Conversations about Race* (New York: Basic Books, 2017), 64. Wendy Anderson likewise explains that white women have supported white nationalism: "White nationalists appropriated terms like feminism, misogyny, sexism, marginalization, revisionist, and alternative voice to ironically offer credence to their claims of white marginalization." Anderson, *Rebirthing a Nation*, 58.

67. Sylvia Wynter, "Beyond Miranda's Meanings: Un/Silencing the 'Demonic Ground' of Caliban's 'Woman,'" in *Out of the Kumbla: Caribbean Women and Literature*, ed. Carole Boyce Davies and Elaine Savory Fido (Trenton, NJ: Africa World Press, 1990), 355–72.

68. Sylvia Wynter, "Unsettling the Coloniality of Being/Power/Truth/Freedom: Towards the Human, after Man, Its Overrepresentation—An Argument," *CR: The New Centennial Review* 3, no. 3 (2003): 260.

69. Rafia Zakaria, *Against White Feminism: Notes on Disruption* (New York: W. W. Norton, 2021), 16.

70. Sabine Broeck, *Gender and the Abjection of Blackness* (Albany: State University of New York Press, 2018), 5; see also Ware, *Beyond the Pale*, 57, 107.

71. Broeck, *Gender and the Abjection of Blackness*, 55.

72. Davis, *Women, Race, & Class*, 33–34.

73. Karen Sánchez-Eppler, "Bodily Bonds: The Intersecting Rhetorics of Feminism and Abolition," *Representations* 24 (1988): 29, 31, 33; see also Shirley Samuels, *The Culture of Sentiment: Race, Gender, and Sentimentality in Nineteenth-Century America* (New York: Oxford University Press, 1992), 97.

74. Sylvia Wynter, *"Do Not Call Us Negros": How "Multicultural" Textbooks Perpetuate Racism* (San Francisco: Aspire Books, 1990), 13.

75. Davis, *Women, Race, & Class*, 111–14. In addition, Davis (142) notes that Susan B. Anthony's feminism was a manifestation of embourgeoisement: "Anthony's staunchly feminist position was also a staunch reflection of bourgeois ideology. And it was probably because of the ideology's blinding powers that she failed to realize that working-class women and Black women alike were fundamentally linked to their men by the class exploitation and racist oppression which did not discriminate between the sexes."

76. Davis, 210.

77. Davis, 121, 229.

78. Kimberlé Crenshaw, "Demarginalizing the Intersection of Race and Sex: A Black Feminist Critique of Antidiscrimination Doctrine, Feminist Theory and Antiracist Politics," *University of Chicago Legal Forum* 1 (1989): 139.

79. Patricia Hill Collins, *Black Feminist Thought: Knowledge, Consciousness and the Politics of Empowerment* (New York: Routledge, 2000), 219.

80. Saba Mahmood, *Politics of Piety: The Islamic Revival and the Feminist Subject* (Princeton, NJ: Princeton University Press, 2012), 6. See also Barbara Biesecker, "Coming to Terms with Recent Attempts to Write Women into the History of Rhetoric," *Philosophy & Rhetoric* 25, no. 2 (1992): 140–61.

81. Mahmood, *Politics of Piety*, 9.

82. Mahmood, *Politics of Piety*, 18.

83. Eve Tuck and K. Wayne Yang, "Decolonization Is Not a Metaphor," *Decolonization: Indigeneity, Education & Society* 1, no. 1 (2012): 3.

84. Sara Ahmed, "A Phenomenology of Whiteness," *Feminist Theory* 8, no. 2 (2007): 149–68.

85. Raka Shome, *Diana and Beyond: White Femininity, National Identity, and Contemporary Media Culture* (Urbana: University of Illinois Press, 2014), 73.

86. Ahmed, *Living a Feminist Life*, 41.

Chapter 1. Bitch Feminism

1. Bitch Media, "About Us," accessed October 21, 2020, https://www.bitchmedia.org/about-us. See Courtney Bailey's analysis of *Bitch* magazine, which celebrates the magazine's use of irony and parody to create feminist community: Courtney Bailey, "*Bitch*ing and Talking/Gazing Back: Feminism as Critical Reading," *Women and Language* 26, no. 2 (2003): 1–8.

2. Allison Yarrow, *90s Bitch: Media, Culture, and the Failed Promise of Gender Equality* (New York: HarperCollins, 2018).

3. Sarah Appleton Aguiar, *The Bitch Is Back: Wicked Women in Literature* (Carbondale: Southern Illinois University Press, 2001).

4. Kalene Westmoreland, "'Bitch' and Lilith Fair: Resisting Anger, Celebrating Contradictions," *Popular Music and Society* 25, no. 1–2 (2001): 207.

5. Koa Beck, *White Feminism: From Suffragettes to Influencers and Who They Leave Behind* (London: Simon and Schuster, 2021), 146.

6. Audre Lorde, *Sister Outsider: Essays and Speeches* (Berkeley, CA: Ten Speed Press, 1984), 60.

7. Kyla Schuller, *The Trouble with White Women: A Counterhistory of Feminism* (New York: Bold Type Books, 2021), 9. I also appreciate Schuller's analysis of Alexandria Ocasio-Cortez and the way she is subject to the optimizing trap of relentless work demands, astute communication, and discourse of beauty, all the while pursuing coalitional politics and intersectional feminism. Schuller (235, 242) argues that while Ocasio-Cortez aims for an "intentional vulnerability" that aims to "break the mythology of perfection in people who hold power," it is "us, not Ocasio-Cortez, who fall into the optimizing trap, awaiting perfection on the House floor, Twitter, and Instagram Live. Chances are, we likely place a similar demand on ourselves to maintain flawlessness—though perhaps with just the right amount of endearing vulnerability."

8. Eric Lott, *Love and Theft: Blackface Minstrelsy and the American Working Class* (New York: Oxford University Press, 1995).

9. I thank the anonymous reviewer for this language.

10. Daniel Morley Johnson, "From the Tomahawk Chop to the Road Block: Discourses of Savagism in Whitestream Media," *American Indian Quarterly* 35, no. 1 (2011): 104–34.

11. Kameron Virk and Nesta McGregor, "Blackfishing: The Women Accused of Pretending to Be Black," BBC News, December 5, 2018; and see bell hooks, "Eating the Other: Desire and Resistance," in *Black Looks: Race and Representation*, by bell hooks (Boston: South End Press, 1992), 21–39.

12. W. T. Lhamon, *Raising Cain: Blackface Performance from Jim Crow to Hip Hop* (Cambridge, MA: Harvard University Press, 2000), 132.

13. Patricia Hill Collins, *Black Sexual Politics: African Americans, Gender, and the New Racism* (New York: Routledge, 2004), 123–24.

14. Collins, 179.

15. Joreen [Jo Freeman], *The Bitch Manifesto*, 1968, published as pamphlet by KNOW, Inc., in 1970, posted to *Jo Freeman* (website), accessed February 15, 2023, https://www.jofreeman.com/joreen/bitch.htm. For a brief etymology, see Britt Peterson, "Meet the New Bitch," *Atlantic Monthly*, April 2015, 37.

16. For enslavism, see Sabine Broeck, *Gender and the Abjection of Blackness* (Albany: State University of New York Press, 2018).

17. Vron Ware, *Beyond the Pale: White Women, Racism, and History* (London: Verso, 1992), 94.

18. Jo Freeman, *On the Origins of the Women's Liberation Movement from a Strictly Personal Perspective*, 1995, posted to *Jo Freeman* (website), accessed October 21, 2020, https://www.jofreeman.com/aboutjo/persorg.htm.

19. Freeman; and cf. Angela Davis, *Women, Race, & Class* (New York: Vintage Books, 1983); Louise Michele Newman, *White Women's Rights: The Racial Origins of Feminism in the United States* (New York: Oxford University Press, 1999).

20. Freeman, *On the Origins of the Women's Liberation Movement*.

21. Joreen, *The Bitch Manifesto*.

22. Freeman, *On the Origins of the Women's Liberation Movement*.

23. Joreen, *The Bitch Manifesto*.

24. Eve Tuck and K. Wayne Yang, "Decolonization Is Not a Metaphor," *Decolonization: Indigeneity, Education & Society* 1, no. 1 (2012): 1–40; see also, Tapji Garba and Sara-Maria Sorentino, "Slavery Is a Metaphor: A Critical Commentary on Eve Tuck and K. Wayne Yang's 'Decolonization Is Not a Metaphor,'" *Antipode* 52, no. 3 (2020): 764–82.

25. Broeck, *Gender and the Abjection of Blackness*, 39.

26. Broeck, 108.

27. Joreen, *The Bitch Manifesto*.

28. Joreen.

29. Joreen.

30. Stephanie Jones-Rogers, *They Were Her Property: White Women as Slave Owners in the American South* (New Haven, CT: Yale University Press, 2019), 134–35.

31. Alexander Weheliye, *Habeas Viscus: Racializing Assemblages, Biopolitics, and Black Feminist Theories of the Human* (Durham, NC: Duke University Press, 2014), 126–27.

32. For the video, see "ORIGINAL VIDEO- Bitchy Resting Face," YouTube video, posted May 22, 2013, by Broken People, 2:38, https://www.youtube.com/watch?v=3v98CPXNiSk.

33. Sara Ahmed, *Living a Feminist Life* (Durham, NC: Duke University Press, 2017), 83.

34. Angela McRobbie, *The Aftermath of Feminism: Gender, Culture, and Social Change* (London: Sage, 2009).

35. See Brianna Wiens and Shana MacDonald, "Living Whose Best Life? An Intersectional Feminist Interrogation of Postfeminist #Solidarity in #Selfcare," *NECSUS*, Spring 2021, https://necsus-ejms.org/portfolio/spring-2021_solidarity/.

36. While multiraciality of the actors is often woven into plotlines, their visual representations, and the spatial logics of the text, this multiraciality can still be coded as white, a figuration of a new beginning and a new race. See LeiLani Nishime, "*The Matrix* Trilogy, Keanu Reeves, and Multiraciality at the End of Time," in *Mixed Race Hollywood*, ed. Mary Beltran and Camilla Fojas (New York: New York University Press, 2008), 290–312. Nevertheless, Richie's racial ambiguity both embraces Blackness and renders Blackness as a form of cool refusal.

37. Lott, *Love and Theft*, 5–7.

38. Rafia Zakaria, *Against White Feminism: Notes on Disruption* (New York: W. W. Norton, 2021), 175.

39. Lott, *Love and Theft*, 27.

40. Saba Mahmood, *Politics of Piety: The Islamic Revival and the Feminist Subject* (Princeton, NJ: Princeton University Press, 2012), 166.

41. Mahmood, 193.

Chapter 2. Mean Girl Feminism

1. Audre Lorde, *Sister Outsider: Essays and Speeches* (Berkeley, CA: Ten Speed Press, 1984), 104–5.

2. Roger Simon and Claudia Eppert, "Remembering Obligation: Pedagogy and the Witnessing of Testimony of Historical Trauma," *Canadian Journal of Education* 22, no. 2 (1997): 178.

3. Rafia Zakaria, *Against White Feminism: Notes on Disruption* (New York: W. W. Norton, 2021), 5.

4. Furthermore, their dialogue demonstrates how their interracial relationship was vexed by affective miscalibrations. Rich's theorizations should be reexamined for her performative citation of Lorde in "Compulsory Heterosexuality and Lesbian Existence," widely considered a founding text on heterosexism, patriarchy, and feminist solidarity. In Rich's formulation of lesbian existence and continuum, woman-identified experience involves a kind of "empowering joy" and—here she turns to Lorde's words—"makes us less willing to accept powerlessness, or those other supplied states of being which are not native to me, such as resignation, despair, self-effacement, depression, self-denial." With this citation, rather than productively engaging with Black knowledge and authorship or acknowledging the role of embodiment and intersectionality, Rich uses Lorde to delineate and mark out women-centered experience as essential to the lesbian continuum and feminist solidarity. But in reading this quote in the context of their relational conflicts, we see how Rich's—and other white women's—feminism is premised on accepting subaltern inarticulateness that feminism itself abjectifies. Adrienne Rich, "Compulsory Heterosexuality and Lesbian Existence," *Signs* 5, no. 4 (1980): 650.

5. Alexander Weheliye, *Habeas Viscus: Racializing Assemblages, Biopolitics, and Black Feminist Theories of the Human* (Durham, NC: Duke University Press, 2014), 9, 126.

6. Sara Ahmed, *Living a Feminist Life* (Durham, NC: Duke University Press, 2017), 203.

7. Lauren Berlant, *The Female Complaint: The Unfinished Business of Sentimentality in American Culture* (Durham, NC: Duke University Press, 2008), 267. Berlant (x) also writes: "Feminine realist-sentimentality thrives in *proximity* to the political, occasionally crossing over in political alliance, even more occasionally doing some politics, but most often not, acting as a critical chorus that sees the expression of emotional response and conceptual recalibration as achievement enough."

8. Naomi Wolf, *The Beauty Myth: How Images of Beauty Are Used against Women* (London: Chatto and Windus, 1990).

9. Susan Douglas, *Enlightened Sexism: The Seductive Message That Feminism's Work Is Done* (New York: Henry Holt, 2010); Angela McRobbie, *The Aftermath of Feminism: Gender, Culture, and Social Change* (London: Sage, 2009).

10. McRobbie, *The Aftermath of Feminism*, 18.

11. Jacques Derrida, *Of Grammatology*, trans. Gayatri Chakravorty Spivak (Baltimore, MD: Johns Hopkins University Press, 1997), 145.

12. Derrida, 154.

13. Elizabeth Behm-Morawitz and Dana Mastro, "Mean Girls? The Influence of Gender Portrayals in Teen Movies on Emerging Adults' Gender-Based Attitudes and Beliefs," *Journalism & Mass Communication Quarterly* 85, no. 1 (2008): 141.

14. Rosalind Wiseman, *Queen Bees and Wannabees: Helping Your Daughter Survive Cliques, Gossip, Boyfriends, and Other Realities of Adolescence* (New York: Three Rivers Press, 2002).

15. Douglas, *Enlightened Sexism*, 236.

16. Enrique Alemán Jr., "Through the Prism of Critical Race Theory: Niceness and Latina/o Leadership in the Politics of Education," *Journal of Latinos and Education* 8, no. 4 (2009): 290–311.

17. Martijn Konings, *The Emotional Logic of Capitalism: What Progressives Have Missed* (Stanford, CA: Stanford University Press, 2015), 7.

18. Gus Andrews, "The, Like, Downfall of the English Language: A Fluffy Word with a Hefty Problem" (Summer 2003), in *BITCHfest: Ten Years of Cultural Criticism from the Pages of Bitch Magazine*, ed. Lisa Jervis and Andi Zeisler (New York: Farrar, Straus and Giroux, 2006), 38–42.

19. Ruby Hamad, *White Tears/Brown Scars: How White Feminism Betrays Women of Color* (New York: Catapult, 2020), 239.

20. Berlant, *The Female Complaint*, 234.

21. Douglas, *Enlightened Sexism*, 9.

22. See also Karen Pitcher, "The Staging of Agency in *Girls Gone Wild*," *Critical Studies in Media Communication* 23, no. 3 (2006): 200–218.

23. Douglas, *Enlightened Sexism*, 207 (qtd.), 214–15.

24. See Ronald Walter Greene, "Rhetorical Agency as Communicative Labor," *Philosophy and Rhetoric* 37, no. 3 (2004): 203.

25. Zakaria, *Against White Feminism*, 6, 8.

26. Zakaria, 16.

27. Douglas, *Enlightened Sexism*, 306.

28. See Angela Davis, *Women, Race, & Class* (New York: Vintage Books, 1983); Louise Michele Newman, *White Women's Rights: The Racial Origins of Feminism in the United States* (New York: Oxford University Press, 1999).

29. See note 4.

30. McRobbie, *The Aftermath of Feminism*, 12.

31. Betty Friedan, *The Feminine Mystique* (New York: Norton, 1963), 15–32.

32. It is worth noting that Huffman, who plays Lynette, was convicted and sentenced to fourteen days in prison for her role in the 2019 Admissions Gate, in which she and others bribed university officials and falsified documents to secure their children's admission to prestigious universities.

33. Esther Sanchez-Pardo, *Cultures of the Death Drive: Melanie Klein and Modernist Melancholia* (Durham, NC: Duke University Press, 2003), 345.

34. Konings, *The Emotional Logic of Capitalism*, 105.

35. Konings, 63.

Chapter 3. Power Couple Feminism

1. Maddie Crum, "How Did 'Power Couple' Become the New Standard for Relationship Success?," *Huffington Post* (blog), June 18, 2016, https://www.huffpost.com/topic/power-couple.

2. Jessie Daniels, *Nice White Ladies: The Truth about White Supremacy, Our Role in It, and How We Can Help to Dismantle It* (New York: Seal Press, 2021), 20.

3. Gloria Steinem, *Revolution from Within: A Book of Self-Esteem* (Boston: Little, Brown, 1992), 263.

4. Sarah Banet-Weiser, *Empowered: Popular Feminism and Popular Misogyny* (Durham, NC: Duke University Press, 2018).

5. Koa Beck, *White Feminism: From Suffragettes to Influencers and Who They Leave Behind* (London: Simon and Schuster, 2021), 165.

6. Sheryl Sandberg, *Lean In: Women, Work, and the Will to Lead* (New York: Alfred Knopf, 2013), 163.

7. Sianne Ngai, *Ugly Feelings* (Cambridge, MA: Harvard University Press, 2005), 21, 129.

8. Wendy Brown, *States of Injury: Power and Freedom in Late Modernity* (Princeton, NJ: Princeton University Press, 1995), 59.

9. I want to note that Tina Turner was positioned in a power couple when she was professionally and romantically linked with Ike Turner, who abused her, prompting Tina to leave the relationship.

10. Ngai, *Ugly Feelings*, 128.

11. Ruby Hamad, *White Tears/Brown Scars: How White Feminism Betrays Women of Color* (New York: Catapult, 2020), 88.

12. *Gossip Girl*, developed by Josh Schwartz and Stephanie Savage, aired on the CW Network to a regular audience of 3.5 million viewers. When *Gossip Girl* aired, there was concern over the proliferation of mean girl characters in media. See, e.g., Scott Pierce, "Can You Like a Show with Unlikable Characters?," *Deseret Morning News*, May 27, 2010; Marieke Hardy, "Mean Girls and Boys: Backchat," *Age*, January 29, 2009, 7; Linda Stasi, "'Girl' Crazy: Prep-School Soap Long on Teen Sex & Drinking," *New York Post*, September 18, 2007, 81; John Doyle, "Why They're All Talking about Gossip Girl," *Globe and Mail*, September 18, 2007, R1; Michelle Gillett, "Tacky Teen Heroines," *Berkshire Eagle*, September 11, 2006; Hannah Johnson, "High School Gossip Goes Viral," *Bismarck Tribune*, January 23, 2013, 1A. However, I interpret this concern over mean girl characters as contributing to the kind of moral panic about girls that is discussed by Emily Ryalls, "Demonizing 'Mean Girls' in the News: Was Phoebe Prince 'Bullied to Death'?," *Communication, Culture, & Critique* 5 (2012): 463–81; and Shayla Thiel-Stern, "Femininity Out of Control on the Internet: A Critical Analysis of Media Representations of Gender, Youth, and MySpace.com in International News Discourses," *Girlhood Studies* 2, no. 1 (2009): 20–39.

13. Ngai, *Ugly Feelings*, 33.

14. Michel Foucault, *History of Sexuality*, vol. 3, *The Care of the Self* (New York: Pantheon Books, 1986), 176 and 192 (qtd.), and see 74–76.

15. Angela Willey, *Undoing Monogamy: The Politics of Science and the Possibilities of Biology* (Durham, NC: Duke University Press, 2016).

16. Sabine Broeck, *Gender and the Abjection of Blackness* (Albany: State University of New York Press, 2018), 21.

17. For example, in season 3, when Vanessa says that she wishes that wealthy Lily van der Woodsen (Kelly Rutherford) and Rufus Humphrey (Matthew Settle) were her parents, presumably because they have access to resources that would support her talent and growth, her mother overhears and questions who she is turning into.

18. Emily D. Ryalls, "Ambivalent Aspirationalism in Millennial Postfeminist Culture on *Gossip Girl*," *Communication and Critical/Cultural Studies* 13, no. 2 (2016): 198–213.

19. For the relationship between gossip, gender, and class boundaries, see Giselle Bastin, "The 1970s Gossip Girls: Gossip's Role in the Surveillance and Construction of Female Social Networks in Helen Garner's *Monkey Grip*," *Antipodes* 23, no. 2 (2009): 115–20.

20. Naomi R. Johnson, "Consuming Desires: Consumption, Romance, and Sexuality in Best-Selling Teen Romance Novels, *Women's Studies in Communication* 33 (2010): 59.

21. Ngai, *Ugly Feelings*, 162.

22. Ed Westwick, "The Hot Seat: Ed Westwick," interview, *Time Out*, September 6, 2010.

23. After the *Gossip Girl* series ended, Westwick was accused of rape and sexual assault by multiple women. Abby Gardner, "'Gossip Girl' Star Ed Westwick Accused of Rape," *Glamour*, July 28, 2018.

24. I thank my students from SPCOM 201: Gender and Communication for sharing their knowledge on the *Fifty Shades of Grey* series.

25. Judith Stacey, *In the Name of the Family: Rethinking Family Values in the Postmodern Age* (Boston: Beacon Press, 1997).

26. Daniels, *Nice White Ladies*, 160.

27. Ann Sanchez, *Power Couples in Antiquity: Transversal Perspectives* (London: Routledge, 2021).

28. Loren Glass, "Publicizing the President's Privates," *Postmodern Culture* 9 no. 3 (1999): para. 33.

29. Patrick Jones and Gretchen Soderlund, "The Conspiratorial Mode of American Television: Politics, Public Relations, and Journalism in *House of Cards* and *Scandal*," *American Quarterly* 69, no. 4 (2017): 835.

30. Suzanne Leonard, "'I May Need You, Peter, but You Sure as Hell Need Me Too': Political Marriages in *The Good Wife* and Beyond," *Television & New Media* 18, no. 2 (2017): 134.

31. T. A. Frank, "Look Who's Hitched! The Secret Lives of Washington's Power Couples," *Washington Monthly*, May 2007, 34–43.

32. "Bill and Hillary Clinton: For Still Thinking about Tomorrow," *Foreign Policy* 197 (December 2012): 34.

33. Glass, "Publicizing the President's Privates," para. 35.

34. Melissa Deem, "Scandal, Heteronormative Culture, and the Disciplining of Feminism," *Critical Studies in Media Communication* 16, no. 1 (1999): 90.

35. Kate O'Beirne, "Village Idiot," *National Review* 50, no. 19 (October 12, 1998): 46.

36. See, e.g., Anne Friedman, "First Ladies in Two Modes," *American Prospect* 18, no. 10 (October 2007): 53–54.

37. Erica Jong, "Hillary's Husband Re-Elected: The Clinton Marriage of Politics and Power," *Nation*, November 25, 1996, 15.

38. Lauren Berlant, *The Female Complaint: The Unfinished Business of Sentimentality in American Culture* (Durham, NC: Duke University Press, 2008), 1.

Chapter 4. Global Mother Feminism

1. Rafia Zakaria discusses how the white savior trope is built into the aid industry; see Rafia Zakaria, *Against White Feminism: Notes on Disruption* (New York: W. W. Norton, 2021), 73.

2. Lauren Berlant, *The Female Complaint: The Unfinished Business of Sentimentality in American Culture* (Durham, NC: Duke University Press, 2008), 6.

3. Ruby Hamad, *White Tears/Brown Scars: How White Feminism Betrays Women of Color* (New York: Catapult, 2020), 141.

4. Raka Shome, "'Global Motherhood': The Transnational Intimacies of White Femininity," *Critical Studies in Media Communication* 28, no. 5 (2011): 392, 390.

5. David Blight, *Race and Reunion: The Civil War in American Memory* (Cambridge, MA: Harvard University Press, 2001), 288. See also Seyward Darby, *Sisters in Hate: American Women on the Front Lines of White Nationalism* (New York: Little, Brown, 2020); Shawn Michelle Smith, *American Archives: Gender, Race, and Class in Visual Culture* (Princeton, NJ: Princeton University Press, 1999); Elizabeth Gillespie McRae, *Mothers of Massive Resistance: White Women and the Politics of White Supremacy* (New York: Oxford University Press, 2018).

6. Louise Michele Newman, *White Women's Rights: The Racial Origins of Feminism in the United States* (New York: Oxford University Press, 1999), 19–20.

7. Zakaria, *Against White Feminism*, 178.

8. Zakaria, 81.

9. Kyla Schuller, *The Trouble with White Women: A Counterhistory of Feminism* (New York: Bold Type Books, 2021), 156.

10. Maureen Dowd describes Palin as the queen bee among the "Republican Mean Girls" of Sharron Angle, Michele Bachmann, Christine O'Donnell, and many other rising conservatives. See Maureen Dowd, "Playing All the Angles," *New York Times*, October 17, 2010. See also David Talbot, "Mean Girl," *Salon*, September 23, 2008; Sarah Jones, "Petty Palin Can't Let Go of Her Mean Girl Ways," PoliticusUSA, August 9, 2010, https://www.politicususa.com/2010/08/09/; Juan Cole, "Rambo and the Mean Girl," *Informed Comment*, September 5, 2008, https://www.juancole.com/; Doug Mataconis, "Conservative Pundits Finally Seeing Sarah Palin for What She Is," *Outside the Beltway*, January 28, 2015, https://www.outsidethebeltway.com/.

11. Shome, "Global Motherhood," 402.

12. Zakaria, *Against White Feminism*, 58.

13. Michael Cooper, "Palin, on Offensive, Attacks Obama's Ties to '60s Radical," *New York Times*, October 4, 2008.

14. Carol Anderson states that white rage began during the presidential campaign with a sharp increase in threats to Obama and "frenzied" Palin rallies; see Carol Anderson, *White Rage: The Unspoken Truth of Our Racial Divide* (New York: Bloomsbury, 2016), 156. On Palin's reality show, see Nancy Franklin, "Mush! Sarah Palin Takes Us for a Ride," *New Yorker*, November 15, 2010.

15. Joanna Weiss, "Sarah Palin, the Cynical Mean Girl," *Boston Globe*, November 21, 2009.

16. Ruth Rosen, "The Tea Party and Angry White Women," *Dissent* 59, no. 1 (2012): 61.

17. Linda Hirshman, "Sarah Palin, Mean Girl," *Nation*, October 20, 2008.

18. Wendy Anderson, *Rebirthing a Nation: White Women, Identity Politics, and the Internet* (Jackson: University Press of Mississippi, 2021), 82.

19. Bruce E. Gronbeck, "Negative Narratives in 1988 Presidential Campaign Ads," *Quarterly Journal of Speech* 78 (1992): 335; Bruce E. Gronbeck and Arthur H. Miller, "Images of the Voter-Citizen in Presidential Campaigns," in *Presidential Campaigns*

and American Self Images, ed. Arthur H. Miller and Bruce E. Gronbeck (New York: Routledge, 1994), 156.

20. Gronbeck, "Negative Narratives in 1988 Presidential Campaign Ads."

21. Kathleen Hall Jamieson, *Dirty Politics: Deception, Distraction, and Democracy* (New York: Oxford University Press, 1992), 212, 52–53 (qtd.).

22. Arthur H. Miller and Bruce E. Gronbeck, "Presidential Campaign Politics at the Crossroads," in Miller and Gronbeck, *Presidential Campaigns and American Self Images*, 258.

23. For a discussion of how political ads and discourse about Willie Horton circulated fear about Black masculinity, see Jessie Daniels, *White Lies: Race, Class, Gender, and Sexuality in White Supremacist Discourse* (New York: Routledge, 1997), 94.

24. Gronbeck, "Negative Narratives in 1988 Presidential Campaign Ads."

25. Dale L. Sullivan, "The Ethos of Epideictic Encounter," *Philosophy and Rhetoric* 26, no. 2 (1993): 124.

26. Maureen Dowd, "Some Like It Highbrow," *Times*, July 24, 2012, 4–5.

27. Laurie Ouellette, "Branding the Right: The Affective Economy of Sarah Palin," *Cinema Journal* 51, no. 4 (2012): 186.

28. Jeffrey Broxmeyer, "Of Politicians, Populism, and Plates: Marketing the Body Politic," *Women's Studies Quarterly* 38, no. 3/4 (2010): 147.

29. Rebecca Traister, *Big Girls Don't Cry: The Election That Changed Everything for America* (New York: Free Press, 2010), 272.

30. Anna Holmes and Rebecca Traister, "A Palin of Our Own," *New York Times*, August 29, 2010, 9.

31. Traister, *Big Girls Don't Cry*, 236; Rebecca Traister, "5 Myths about Female Candidates," *Washington Post*, October 31, 2010, B05. See also Jack Kelly, "Hate Mongers: The Media Is Misrepresenting McCain-Palin Rallies," *Pittsburgh Post-Gazette*, October 19, 2008, G3.

32. Colleen Carroll Campbell, "The Palin Effect," *St. Louis Post-Dispatch*, June 17, 2010, A15.

33. Kathleen Parker, "Mean Girls?," *Washington Post*, October 20, 2010, A17.

34. Sarah Palin, *Going Rogue: An American Life* (New York: HarperCollins, 2009), 253, 283, 352.

35. Palin, 235–37, 335, 370 (qtd.); see also Ben Boychuk and Joel Mathis, "*Going Rogue* Renews Attacks on Both Sides," *Korea Times*, November 23, 2009.

36. Palin, *Going Rogue*, 230, 236, 272, 283.

37. On the notion of political haves and have-nots, see Karen Johnson-Cartee and Gary Copeland, *Negative Political Advertising: Coming of Age* (Hillsdale, NJ: Lawrence Erlbaum, 1991), 107–18.

38. See Johnson-Cartee and Copeland, 65; Jamieson, *Dirty Politics*, 81; and (more generally) McRae, *Mothers of Massive Resistance*.

39. Zakaria, *Against White Feminism*, 79–80.

40. Palin, *Going Rogue*, 3.

41. McRae, *Mothers of Massive Resistance*, 7.

42. Fiona McIntosh, "Supermom Captures the Heart of America," *Daily Mirror*, September 7, 2008, 25.

43. Jessie Daniels, *Nice White Ladies: The Truth about White Supremacy, Our Role in It, and How We Can Help to Dismantle It* (New York: Seal Press, 2021), 163.

44. Jeanette J. Lee, "Alaska Chooses Grizzly for State Quarter," *Seattle Times*, April 24, 2007.

45. W. Anderson, *Rebirthing a Nation*, 91.

46. Robert Dillon, "Alaska Governor Talks Gas Line, Polar Bear Woes on Capitol Hill," *Natural Gas Week* 24, no. 9 (March 3, 2008): 4; Julie J. Bosman, "Provoking Palin's Inner Bear," *New York Times*, October 19, 2008, https://www.nytimes.com/.

47. Bruce E. Gronbeck, "Character, Celebrity, and Sexual Innuendo in the Mass-Mediated Presidency," in *Media Scandals*, ed. James Lull and Stephen Hinerman (New York: Columbia University Press, 1997), 141.

48. Koa Beck, *White Feminism: From Suffragettes to Influencers and Who They Leave Behind* (London: Simon and Schuster, 2021), 161.

49. "Mrs. Bush's Interview on the Tonight Show with Jay Leno," transcript, *George W. Bush White House* (website), April 26, 2005, https://georgewbush-whitehouse.archives.gov/; Michael A. Fletcher, "First Lady a 'Critical Asset' at Republican Fundraisers," *Washington Post*, August 16, 2006.

50. Molly Meijer Wertheimer, "Laura Bush: Using the 'Magic of Words' to Educate and Advocate," in *Inventing a Voice: The Rhetoric of American First Ladies of the Twentieth Century*, ed. Molly Meijer Wertheimer (Lanham, MD: Rowman and Littlefield, 2004), 444.

51. Ronald Kessler, *Laura Bush: An Intimate Portrait of the First Lady* (New York: Doubleday, 2006), 8. According to Laura J. Shepherd, the discursive links that were established at this time between al-Qaeda and the Taliban strengthened the demonization of the latter, but it was the Taliban (and not al-Qaeda, specifically) that was viewed as espousing antifeminist politics and practices. See Laura J. Shepherd, "Veiled References: Constructions of Gender in the Bush Administration Discourse on the Attacks on Afghanistan Post-9/11," *International Feminist Journal of Politics* 8, no. 1 (2006): 19–41.

52. Zakaria, *Against White Feminism*, 57–59.

53. Hamad, *White Tears/Brown Scars*, 199–200.

54. Michael Dillon and Julian Reid, *The Liberal Way of War: Killing to Make Life Live* (London: Routledge, 2009).

55. Dillon and Reid, 40, 43.

56. Linda Kerber, "The Republican Mother: Women and the Enlightenment—An American Perspective," *American Quarterly* 28, no. 2 (1976): 188.

57. Tasha N. Dubriwny, "First Ladies and Feminism: Laura Bush as Advocate for Women's and Children's Rights," *Women's Studies in Communication* 28, no. 1 (2005): 88.

58. Shawn J. Parry-Giles and Diane M. Blair, "The Rise of the Rhetorical First Lady: Politics, Gender Ideology, and Women's Voice, 1789–2002," *Rhetoric & Public Affairs* 5, no. 4 (2002): 581.

59. Ann Gerhart, *The Perfect Wife: the Life and Choices of Laura Bush* (New York: Simon and Schuster, 2004), 180.

60. Wertheimer, "Laura Bush," 459–61.

61. Hamad, *White Tears/Brown Scars*, 235.

62. Brad Evans, "The Liberal War Thesis: Introducing the Ten Key Principles of Twenty-First-Century Biopolitical Warfare," *South Atlantic Quarterly* 110, no. 3 (2011): 753.

63. Evans, 752.

64. Robert P. Watson, "*Source Material*: Toward the Study of the First Lady: The State of Scholarship," *Presidential Studies Quarterly* 33, no. 2 (2003): 434.

65. Dillon and Reid, *The Liberal Way of War*, 86.

66. Kevin Ayotte and Mary E. Husain, "Securing Afghan Women: Neocolonialism, Epistemic Violence, and the Rhetoric of the Veil," *NWSA Journal* 17, no. 3 (2005): 123.

67. Daniels, *Nice White Ladies,* 78.

68. Dana L. Cloud, "'To Veil the Threat of Terror': Afghan Women and the ⟨Clash of Civilizations⟩ in the Imagery of the U.S. War on Terrorism," *Quarterly Journal of Speech* 90, no. 3 (2006): 292; see also "Mrs. Bush's Remarks at USAID Event with Afghan Authority Interim Chairman Karzai," transcript, *George W. Bush White House* (website), January 29, 2002, https://georgewbush-whitehouse.archives.gov/.

69. In 2012, while on her way home from school, Malala Yousafzai was shot in the head by a Taliban gunman. She survived, coauthored a memoir in 2013 to tell her story to a global audience, and was awarded the Nobel Peace Prize in 2014. In addition to featuring her story, the Western news media regularly publishes accounts of violence in and around the establishment of schools for girls and women in Afghanistan. See, e.g., Mishal Husain, "Malala: The Girl Who Was Shot for Going to School," *BBC News*, October 7, 2013, https://www.bbc.com/; Masoud Popalzai, "Official: 160 Girls Poisoned at Afghan School," *CNN*, May 29, 2012, https://www.cnn.com/.

70. Evans, "The Liberal War Thesis," 749. See also Kristin L. Hoganson, *Fighting for American Manhood: How Gender Politics Provoked the Spanish-American and Philippine-American Wars* (New Haven, CT: Yale University Press, 1998); Iris Marion Young, "The Logic of Masculinist Protection: Reflections on the Current Security State," *Signs: Journal of Women in Culture and Society* 29, no. 1 (2003): 1–25.

71. For a critique of smart war technologies, see, e.g., Scott Peterson, "'Smarter' Bombs Still Hit Civilians," *Christian Science Monitor*, October 22, 2002.

72. Miriam Ticktin, "Sexual Violence as the Language of Border Control: Where French Feminist and Anti-Immigrant Rhetoric Meet," *Signs: Journal of Women in Culture and Society* 33, no. 4 (2008): 863–89; Madhavi Sunder, "Piercing the Veil," *Yale Law Journal* 112, no. 6 (2003): 1399–472.

73. The role of the United States in various conflicts in Afghanistan is well described in Charles Hirschkind and Saba Mahmood, "Feminism, the Taliban, and Politics of Counter-Insurgency," *Anthropological Quarterly* 75, no. 2 (2002): 339–54.

74. "Mrs. Laura Bush's Leadership," fact sheet, *George W. Bush White House* (website), January 12, 2012, https://georgewbush-whitehouse.archives.gov/. See also, at the same website: "Mrs. Bush's Remarks at the Kabul Presidential Palace," transcript, June 9, 2008; "Mrs. Bush's Remarks at Conference of the National Association of Women Judges," transcript, October 10, 2003.

75. "Mrs. Bush's Remarks on International Women's Day at the United Nations," transcript, *George W. Bush White House* (website), March 8, 2002, https://georgewbush-whitehouse.archives.gov/. See also, at the same website: "Mrs. Bush Delivers Remarks at the World Economic Forum," transcript, May 21, 2005; "Mrs. Bush's Remarks at Conference of Women Leaders, International Women's Day Event," transcript, March 8, 2005; "Mrs. Bush's Remarks at the 2004 Fortune Most Powerful Women Summit," transcript, October 6, 2004.

76. "Interview of the First Lady by Dalia Al-Aqidi of Al Hurra Middle East Television on International Women's Day," transcript, *George W. Bush White House* (website), March 8, 2004. https://georgewbush-whitehouse.archives.gov/.

77. According to the Revolutionary Association of the Women of Afghanistan (RAWA), textbooks in Afghanistan were paid for by Unocal, a US oil company, and then reprinted by the US Agency for International Development (USAID). See RAWA, "Educational Opportunities Are Not Improving for Afghan Women," in *Afghanistan: Opposing Viewpoints*, ed. John Woodward (Farmington Hills, MI: Greenhaven Press, 2006), 80–85.

78. "Interview of Mrs. Bush by Meredith Viera, NBC 'Today' Show," transcript, *George W. Bush White House* (website), September 18, 2006, https://georgewbush-whitehouse.archives.gov/. See also, at the same website: "Mrs. Bush's Remarks at the White House Symposium on Advancing Global Literacy: Building a Foundation for Freedom," transcript, September 22, 2008.

79. Maria Raha, "Veiled Intentions: The U.S. Media's Hug and Run Affair with Afghan Women," in *The W Effect: Bush's War on Women*, ed. Laura Flanders (New York: Feminist Press, 2004), 179.

80. Mimi Thi Nguyen, "The Biopower of Beauty: Humanitarian Imperialisms and Global Feminisms in an Age of Terror," *Signs: Journal of Women in Culture and Society* 36, no. 2 (2011): 367.

81. Minh-Ha Pham, "The Right to Fashion in the Age of Terrorism," *Signs: Journal of Women in Culture and Society* 36, no. 2 (2011): 390.

82. "Mrs. Bush's Remarks at Women Leaders Luncheon in Hungary," transcript, *George W. Bush White House* (website), May 17, 2002, https://georgewbush-whitehouse.archives.gov/.

83. As Eva Chen argues, choice about clothing and consumption is seen as constitutive of agency. See Eva Chen, "Neoliberal Self-Governance and Popular Postfeminism

in Contemporary Anglo-American Chick Lit," *Concentric: Literary and Cultural Studies* 36, no. 1 (2010): 243–75.

84. Meyda Yeğenoğlu, *Colonial Fantasies: Towards a Feminist Reading of Orientalism* (Cambridge: Cambridge University Press, 1998), 107.

85. Saba Mahmood, *Politics of Piety: The Islamic Revival and the Feminist Subject* (Princeton, NJ: Princeton University, 2005), 180.

86. Nadje Sadig Al-Ali and Nicola Christine Pratt, *What Kind of Liberation? Women and the Occupation of Iraq* (Berkeley: University of California Press, 2009), 9–10.

87. Samira Ahmed, "G2 Women: Raising Hope," *Guardian*, October 7, 2011, 14.

88. Mariella Frostrup, "Women's Rights In, Before Troops Out," *Times*, October 8, 2011; see also Kathleen Parker, "Why Those 'Pet Rocks' Matter in Afghanistan and Beyond," *Washington Post*, April 3, 2011, A21; Kathleen Parker, "Afghanistan's Real Gold," *Washington Post*, June 16, 2010, A17; Aryn Baker, "Afghan Women and the Return of the Taliban," *Time*, August 9, 2010, 23.

89. Krista Hunt, "'Embedded Feminism' and the War on Terror," in *(En)Gendering the War on Terror: War Stories and Camouflaged Politics*, ed. Krista Hunt and Kim Rygiel (Hampshire: Ashgate, 2006), 51–71.

90. Jennifer L. Fluri, "Feminist Nation-Building in Afghanistan: An Examination of the Revolutionary Association of the Women of Afghanistan (RAWA)," *Feminist Review* 89, no. 1 (2008): 38.

91. Dillon and Reid, *The Liberal Way of War*, 147.

92. See Achilles Mbembe, "Necropolitics," *Public Culture* 15, no. 1 (2003): 11–40.

93. Newman, *White Women's Rights*, 53.

94. Newman, 166.

95. Beck, *White Feminism*, 172.

Conclusion. Abolishing Mean Girl Feminism

1. Rafia Zakaria, *Against White Feminism: Notes on Disruption* (New York: W. W. Norton, 2021), 103.

2. Sara Ahmed, "A Phenomenology of Whiteness," *Feminist Theory* 8, no. 2 (2007): 149–68.

3. Lauren Berlant, *The Female Complaint: The Unfinished Business of Sentimentality in American Culture* (Durham, NC: Duke University Press, 2008), xii.

4. Kyla Schuller, *The Trouble with White Women: A Counterhistory of Feminism* (New York: Bold Type Books, 2021), 257.

5. Sara Ahmed, *Complaint!* (Durham, NC: Duke University Press, 2021), 254.

6. Paul Gilroy, "'We Got to Get Over before We Go Under . . .': Fragments for a History of Black Vernacular Neoliberalism," *New Formations: A Journal of Culture/Theory/Politics* 80 (2013): 34.

7. Gabrielle Union, "Dear Isis," *Cut*, September 14, 2021, https://www.thecut.com/2021/09/dear-isis-book-excerpt-from-gabrielle-union.html; and see Gabrielle Union, *You Got Anything Stronger?* (New York: HarperCollins, 2021).

8. Enrique Alemán Jr., "Through the Prism of Critical Race Theory: Niceness and Latina/o Leadership in the Politics of Education," *Journal of Latinos and Education* 8, no. 4 (2009): 306.

9. Ahmed, *Complaint!*; Patricia Hill Collins, *Black Sexual Politics: African Americans, Gender, and the New Racism* (New York: Routledge, 2004), 123–24.

10. Karen Potts and Leslie Brown, "Becoming an Anti-Oppressive Researcher," in *Research as Resistance: Critical, Indigenous, and Anti-Oppressive Approaches*, ed. Susan Strega and Leslie Brown (Toronto: Canadian Scholars' Press, 2005), 255–86.

11. Sara Ahmed, *Living a Feminist Life* (Durham, NC: Duke University Press, 2017), 255 (emphasis added).

12. Glen Coulthard, *Red Skin, White Masks: Rejecting the Colonial Politics of Recognition* (Minneapolis: University of Minnesota Press, 2014), 133.

13. Coulthard, 147.

14. Ruby Hamad, *White Tears/Brown Scars: How White Feminism Betrays Women of Color* (New York: Catapult, 2020), 196.

15. LeRhonda Manigault-Bryant, "An Open Letter to White Liberal Feminists," *Black Perspectives* (blog), African American Intellectual History Society, November 19, 2016, https://www.aaihs.org/an-open-letter-to-white-liberal-feminists/.

16. Jacquelyn Dowd Hall, *Revolt against Chivalry: Jessie Daniel Ames and the Women's Campaign against Lynching* (New York: Columbia University Press, 1979), 194, 167.

17. Hall, 163, 194, 221 (qtd.).

18. Vron Ware, *Beyond the Pale: White Women, Racism, and History* (London: Verso, 1992), 253.

19. Ahmed, *Living a Feminist Life*, 260.

20. Koa Beck, *White Feminism: From Suffragettes to Influencers and Who They Leave Behind* (London: Simon and Schuster, 2021), 235.

21. Zakaria, *Against White Feminism*, 58.

22. bell hooks, *Feminist Theory: From Margin to Center* (London: Pluto Press, 2000).

23. Stacey Waite, "Cultivating the Scavenger: A Queerer Feminist Future for Composition and Rhetoric," *Peitho* 18, no. 1 (2015), https://cfshrc.org/article/cultivating-the-scavenger-a-queerer-feminist-future-for-composition-and-rhetoric/.

Index

Abedin, Huma, 72
Accapadi, Mamta Motwani, 8
accountability, 44, 71, 96, 98–99, 101
Afghanistan, 83, 86–89, 119n51, 120n69, 121n77
Afghan women, 76, 83–84, 86–89, 121n77
Agamben, Giorgio, 12, 108n54
agency: and bitch feminism, 20, 26, 29, 34; and dress or fashion, 88, 121n83; and mean girl feminism, 3; and post-feminism, 43, 51; and power couple feminism, 59–60, 67–69; and racialized meanness, 97; and white feminism, 5, 18–19, 92; and white womanhood, 19, 94
Aguiar, Sarah Appleton, 26
Ahmed, Sara: on feminism, 6, 13, 36, 43, 95, 105n5; on feminist killjoys, xii, 22, 97, 99; on nonperformativity, 7; and whiteness, 20
Alemán, Enrique, Jr., 97
al-Qaeda, 76, 87, 119n51. See also Afghanistan
Ames, Jessie Daniel, 98–99
Anderson, Wendy, 9, 78, 82, 108n66
anger: and bitch feminism, 27, 31; and Black womanhood, 96; and feminism, 101; and mean girl feminism, ix, x, xii, 12, 20–21, 23, 41, 94; and mobilization, ix; and white feminism, vii
Anthony, Susan B., 10, 17, 109n75
anti-Blackness, 16, 20, 40. See also Blackness

articulation: and feminism, 42–43, 95, 97; and mean girl feminism, ix, x, 8, 20, 22, 44, 46, 48–50, 55, 57; and rage, 45, 53–54; and white feminism, ix, xii, 6, 21, 52, 112n4
Association of Southern Women for the Prevention of Lynching (ASWPL), 98–99
Azalea, Iggy, 28

Banet-Weiser, Sarah, 60, 104n12
beauty, 29, 41, 44–45, 49, 51, 56, 80, 87–89, 92
Beauvoir, Simone de, 32
Beck, Koa, viii, xii, xiii, 3–5, 9–10, 26, 90, 100
Behm-Morawitz, Elizabeth, 46
Berlant, Lauren, xi, 14, 43, 71, 75, 94, 113n7
biopolitics, 76–77, 81, 83–89, 93
biopower, 22, 73, 75–77, 90, 93
Birth of a Nation, The (1915), 15, 108n64
bitch/Bitch feminism, 20, 25–26, 40, 92; and Bitch Manifesto, 19, 29–34; and blackface, 27–28, 33–35, 39–40; and enslavism, 20, 29–30, 32–33, 40; future of, 40–41; and Good News, 36–39; and mean girl feminism, 12, 20, 51, 99; vs. racialized meanness, 97; and RBF, 34–36
Bitch Manifesto, The (Joreen), ix, 19–20, 27, 29–34, 40, 92, 96
"Bitchy Resting Face," 20, 27, 34–36, 40
blackface, 20, 27–29, 33–35, 39–40

Black feminism, 9, 22, 27

Black Lives Matter, 98

Blackness: and bitch feminism, 20, 39–40; and blackface, 27–28, 34; and mean girl feminism, 3, 48, 57; and multiraciality, 112n36; in popular culture, 29; and white feminism, 16, 52, 56

Black people, 9, 17–18, 20, 28, 30, 32, 61, 81, 86

Black women/womanhood: and bitch feminism, 25, 27–30, 33–36, 40, 92; erasure of, 8, 17–18, 27; and Joreen, 20, 31–32; and meanness, 95–97

Bluest Eye, The (Morrison), 22

"Boardroom Bitch," 27, 34, 36–37

bodies: and bitch feminism, 32, 38, 51; and mean girl feminism, 14, 16, 55, 93–94; and postfeminism, 44, 50; and power couple feminism, 65, 71; and white feminism, 4, 11, 17, 51–52, 80, 91–92, 98–99. *See also* embodiment

Boushie, Colten, 15

Bring It On, 96

Broeck, Sabine, 8, 16–17, 32, 63

Broken People, 27, 34–35

Brooks, Meredith, 26

Brown, Wendy, 8, 13, 60

Broxmeyer, Jeffrey, 79

burqas, 87–88. *See also* Afghan women

Burstein, Nanette, 70

Bush, Laura, 22, 76, 82–90, 93

Butler, Judith, 5, 19

Campbell, Colleen Carroll, 80

capitalism: and bitch feminism, 37–38; and feminism, 52, 56; and global mother feminism, 85–87; and mean girl feminism, 3, 53; and power couple feminism, 59, 67; and racialized meanness, 95; and white feminism, 6, 18, 44, 98

celebrities, 1–2, 28, 59–60, 65, 69, 75

cis-heteropatriarchy: and bitch feminism, 26, 29, 33, 36; and illegible rage, 53; and mean girl feminism, x, 3, 20, 22–23, 41, 54, 92; and postfeminism, 43, 52; and power couple feminism, 21, 59, 61–63, 68, 72; and racialized mean girls, 95; and white feminism, 6–7, 10, 14–15, 18, 20, 22, 91

civility: and bitch feminism, 34, 40; and knowledge, 42; and mean girl feminism, xi, 3, 14, 20, 23, 41, 46–48, 57; and postfeminism, 21; and power couple

feminism, 14, 57; and rudeness, 108n54; and white feminism, 8–15, 19, 22

civil rights movement, 20, 30–31, 70

Cixous, Hélène, 4

class: and bitch, usage of, 28–29; and civility, 12; and colonialism, 10; in *Gossip Girl*, 64–65, 115n17; and liberal war, 88; and mean girl feminism, 48, 51; and political campaigns, 79; and Sarah Palin, 77; and white feminism, 14, 76, 109n75; and white womanhood, viii, 9, 11, 89

Clinton, Bill, 61–62, 69–73

Clinton, Hillary, 61–62, 69–73, 84, 98

Cloud, Dana L., 86

Clueless, 49–50

collective action, ix, 94–95, 97, 99

Collins, Patricia Hill, 18, 27, 29, 40, 97, 99

colonialism: and civility, 12; and global mother feminism, 75–76, 81, 89–90; and mean girl feminism, 2, 23, 57; and metaphor, 32; and monogamy, 63; and racialized meanness, 97; and violence, culture of, 3–4; and white feminism, 6, 19–20, 22, 93, 98; and white womanhood, 1, 10–11, 16, 89–90

Combahee River Collective, xi

communication strategies: and bitch feminism, 26, 35–36, 92; and global mother feminism, 81; and mean girl feminism, 2, 11, 22; and neoliberalism, 3; in politics, 78–79; and white feminism, 5, 13, 18, 43–44, 46

community: and bitch feminism, 40, 97; and decolonial feminism, 100–101; and global mother feminism, 87, 89; and mean girl feminism, xii; and performativity, 7; and power couple feminism, 21, 59–60, 93

conservative feminism, 73, 76–77, 79, 89–90

conservativism: and Laura Bush, 82; and global mother feminism, 22, 77; and Hillary Clinton, 70–71; and motherhood, 84; and Nguyen, 100; and nuclear families, 68; and Sarah Palin, 76, 80; and white feminism, 19, 22, 90

Coulthard, Glen, 97

Crash, 53–54, 56, 96

Crenshaw, Kimberlé, 18

damsel in distress, 2, 4, 7, 16, 91–92

Daniels, Jessie, 6–7, 14, 85, 108n60

Davetian, Benet, 12, 108n54

Freeman, Jo (Joreen), ix, 20, 27, 29–34, 70
Friedan, Betty, 54–55, 70
Frostrup, Mariella, 88

Garner, Eric, viii
gender: and bitch feminism, 20, 26–27, 32–33, 37–38, 40; and Laura Bush, 85; and civility, 12; and Hillary Clinton, 70–71; and *Clueless*, 50; and colonialism, 10–11; and decolonial feminism, 100–101; and enslavism, 17; and feminism, 2–8; and global mother feminism, 22, 75–77, 89, 93; and mean girl feminism, 2–3, 21, 41, 49, 54–57, 64, 91–92; and *Mean Girls*, 48; and Sarah Palin, 78–82; in popular culture, xi, 66; and post-feminism, 43–45, 56; and power couple feminism, 72; and white feminism, 7, 16, 18–19, 45, 52, 91, 94, 98–99; and white womanhood, 5, 98
gender studies, 2, 5–6, 8, 14, 16–17, 20, 25–26, 44, 93
girlbossing: and bitch feminism, 34, 37–39, 92; and documentation, 42; explanation, vii; and feminism, xii, 99; and mean girl feminism, 7–8, 23, 49, 57, 92; and power couple feminism, 68; and white feminism, ix–x; and white womanhood, 16
Glass, Loren, 70
global capitalism, 52–53, 56, 87
global mother feminism, 14, 21–22, 73–77; and Laura Bush, 76, 82–89, 93; vs. racialized meanness, 96; and Sarah Palin, 76–82, 89, 93; and white feminism, 8, 93; and white womanhood, 75, 77, 89–90
Going Rouge (Palin), 77–78, 80–81
Gossip Girl, 5, 16, 61–68, 115n12
grassroots feminism, 77, 83, 100
Great News, 20, 27, 34, 36–40, 92
Greene, Ronald Walter, 51
Gregg, Melissa, 3
Grier, Pam, 29
Grimké, Angelina, 17
Gronbeck, Bruce E., 78, 82

Halberstam, Jack, 8
Hamad, Ruby, 5, 7, 9, 50, 61, 75, 83–84, 105n5
heteronormativity: and bitch feminism, 36; and feminism, 5, 7; and global mother feminism, 76; and mean girl feminism, 2–3, 20, 92–93; and post-

feminism, 41, 44–45; and power couple feminism, 21, 57, 59–61, 63; and white feminism, 10, 18, 27, 91
heterosexism, x, 1–2, 5, 26, 67, 112n4
heterosexuality: and global mother feminism, 75, 79; and marriage, 63, 70; and power couple feminism, ix, 8, 21, 58–62, 93; and white feminism, 6, 16, 19
heterosociality, 8, 60, 65–66, 68, 72–73, 93
Hill, Anita, 26
Hillary, 62, 70–72
Hirshman, Linda, 78
holistic approach, 90
Hollis, Rachel, x
Holmes, Anna, 80
hooks, bell, 101, 104n14, 108n64
Horton, Willie, 79, 118n23
hostility, 48, 50, 60–61, 65, 72, 80–81, 96
Huffman, Felicity, 55, 114n32
humanitarianism, 83, 85, 87, 89

identity and subjectivity: and bitch feminism, 28, 33, 37, 40–41; and civility, 13–14; and feminism, xii, 5, 7, 18, 101; and global mother feminism, 75, 77, 84; and mean girl feminism, 2, 21, 51, 99; and white feminism, 16, 19, 42–43, 94; and white womanhood, 46
imperialism, 4, 69, 75, 84, 93
imperialist white supremacist capitalist cis-heteropatriarchy: and bitch, usage of, 20; and global mother feminism, 77, 82; and mean girl feminism, 2–3, 45, 49, 95; and people of color, 58; and power couple feminism, 21, 93; usage of term, 104n14; and white feminism, 18, 92, 94; and white womanhood, xii
Indigenous peoples, 10–11, 15, 27, 89
individualism, 3, 19, 36, 92, 94, 99
infantile citizenship, 79
"Inner White Girl," vii
innocence: and bitch feminism, 30; and feminism, 101; and mean girl feminism, xii, 2, 7, 14, 48, 99; and white feminism, 19–20, 45; and white womanhood, viii, 108n60
intelligibility, 6, 13–14, 17, 43, 45–46, 60–61
intersectionality: and feminism, 95; and illegible rage, 53; and racialized meanness, 96–97; and white feminism, ix, xii–xiii, 18, 30, 44, 92; and white womanhood, xi
invasion and intervention, 76, 83, 86–88

Ireland, Patricia, 70

Jamieson, Kathleen Hall, 78
Johnson, Daniel Morley, 28
Johnson, Naomi R., 65
Jones, Cecily, 11
Jones, Leslie, vii, viii
Jones, Patrick, 69
Jones-Rogers, Stephanie, 9, 34
Jong, Erica, 70
Joreen (Jo Freeman), ix, 20, 27, 29–34, 70
justice, 13, 30, 56–57, 60, 90, 95–96

Karen meme, vii–viii, ix, 15–16, 55
Kerber, Linda, 84
Key & Peele, 58, 62
King, Coretta Scott, 31
King, Martin Luther, Jr., 30, 70
Kipnis, Laura, 8–9
knowledge, 18, 22, 42–43, 57, 79, 86, 112n4

La Rue, Linda, 31
Lean In (Sandberg), 4, 60
Leonard, Suzanne, 69
lesbian existence, 42–43, 112n4
Lhamon, W. T., 28
liberal feminism: critique of, 2; and global mother feminism, 22, 76–77, 89–90, 93; and mean girl feminism, 49, 57; and postfeminism, 41, 45, 79–80; and white womanhood, 4, 8, 95
liberalism: and blackfishing, 28; and global motherhood, 22; and Laura Bush, 82–86; and racism, 3–4; and Sarah Palin, 77, 80–81; and War on Terror, 76, 86; and white feminism, 90; and white womanhood, vii, 49
liberal war, 83–89
liberation: and bitch feminism, 33; and liberal war, 88–89; and mean girl feminism, ix, x, 6–8, 23, 57, 91; and racialized meanness, 97; and white feminism, 16, 20, 27, 52, 92
literacy, 84, 86–87. *See also* education
Little, 95–96
Little Fires Everywhere, 74–75, 96
Lorde, Audre, 6, 27, 42–43, 52, 57, 112n4
Lott, Eric, 27–28, 39–40
love and intimacy: and global mother feminism, 75, 81–82; in *Gossip Girl*, 63–68; and monogamy, 63; and power couple feminism, 21, 57, 59–63, 70–73, 93

lynching, 98–99

Mahmood, Saba, 19, 41
male gaze: and bitch feminism, 33; and mean girl feminism, 2, 45–47, 49–50, 53, 60, 92; and postfeminism, 20, 44; and white feminism, 41, 98
marginalized groups, x–xi, 2, 6, 18, 43, 49–50, 90, 97
marriage, 17, 21, 59–60, 62–63, 65, 67–72
masculinity, 1–2, 21, 37, 61, 68, 93, 105n5
masquerade, feminine, 44, 53
Mastro, Dana, 46
maternalism, 75, 83
McCain, John, 77, 80–81
McEwan, Melissa, 6, 79–80
McRae, Elizabeth Gillespie, 9
McRobbie, Angela, 37, 44–45, 51–53, 56
"Mean" (Swift), 1–2, 7, 14, 18
mean girl feminism, viii, 1–2; abolition of, 91–101; and bitch feminism, 12, 20, 51, 99; and civility, xi, 4, 14, 20, 23, 41, 46–48, 57; and embourgeoisement, 2, 11, 18, 48–49, 62, 64, 66–67; and feminist scholarship, 50–56, 60; and global mother feminism, 76, 81; history and theoretical context, 3–8; and illegible rage, 49, 51, 53–55, 92; and Sarah Palin, 77–78; and performativity, xii, 2–3, 7, 14, 22–23, 46, 49, 53, 55–57, 91–94, 99; and postfeminism, 6, 20–21, 41, 43–44, 46, 50–51; and power couple feminism, 8, 61, 68, 72; vs. racialized meanness, 95–97; and white womanhood, xii, 1–3, 13–14, 23, 49, 54, 57, 91–94
Mean Girls, 5, 20–21, 45–50, 56–57, 92, 96
mean girl trope: in feminist scholarship, 21, 41, 53; in *Gossip Girl*, 64, 115n12; in *Mean Girls*, 20, 45–47, 49; and Sarah Palin, 22; and power couple feminism, 59, 61–63, 69; and white feminism, 46, 56; and women of color, 95–96
meanness: vs. anger, ix–x; and bitch feminism, 14, 26, 33–35, 39–40, 92; and civility, 12–14, 20; and feminism, xi, 3–4, 6–8, 14, 22, 60, 94; and feminism vs. postfeminism, 21, 41, 45, 47, 49–52, 57, 93; and global mother feminism, 14, 81; in *Gossip Girl*, 64–65; and knowledge, 42; and mean girl feminism, 46, 91; in *Mean Girls*, 20–21, 45, 47–49; and Sarah Palin, 76–78, 80; and performativity, 7, 55, 95; in popular culture, 1–2, 22;

meanness (*continued*): and power couple feminism, 14, 61; racialized, 22, 95–98, 101; and white feminism, viii, xii–xiii, 15–16, 21, 45, 49, 94; and white womanhood, xi, 2, 40, 57, 108n60

Menon, Vinay, 3

metaphor, 32–33, 74

Miller, Arthur H., 79

minstrel shows, 28, 39. *See also* blackface

monogamy, 59–61, 63–68, 72, 93

morality: and bitch feminism, 33, 40; and global mother feminism, 82, 89; and liberal war, 88–89; and marriage, 63; and mean girl feminism, 2, 18, 65, 92, 115n12; and nuclear families, 68; and power couple feminism, 69; and white feminism, 10–11, 38, 94; and white womanhood, 9, 16, 18

Moss, Gabrielle, 4

mothering and motherhood, ix, 8, 18, 37, 84

Mr. & Mrs. Smith, 37, 66

multiculturalism, 49, 59, 68, 73, 97

Muñoz, José, 5

nationalism, 21, 81–82, 90, 108n66

negative narratives, 78–80, 89

neoliberal feminism, 44, 50, 93, 95

neoliberalism: and bitch feminism, 34–35, 37–40, 92; and feminism, 52; and girl power culture, 104n3; and global mother feminism, 86; and mean girl feminism, 1–3, 8, 23; and monogamy, 63; and Sarah Palin, 81–82; and popular feminism, 104n12; and postfeminism, 50, 56; and power couple feminism, 59–60, 66–67, 72; and white feminism, 18, 92–93

Newman, Louise Michele, 8, 10, 75, 89

news media, 69, 79–81, 120n69

Ng, Celeste, 74

Ngai, Sianne, 61, 66

Nguyen, Mimi Thi, 87

nice girl trope, 21, 41, 45–47

niceness: and bitch feminism, 29–30; and Laura Bush, 22, 76; and civility, 13; and global mother feminism, 77; and mean girl feminism, 99; and racialized meanness, 97; and white womanhood, 4, 11, 104–5n3, 108n60

nonviolence: and civility, 13; and embourgeoisement, 4, 11, 17; and feminism vs.

postfeminism, 45, 48; and global mother feminism, 77, 85–86; and mean girl feminism, 4, 99; and power couple feminism, 63, 93; and white feminism, 14, 22

nuclear families, 4, 68. *See also* families

Nyong'o, Tavia, 13

Obama, Barack, 52, 77, 117n14

O'Beirne, Kate, 70

Ocasio-Cortez, Alexandria, 25, 40–41, 110n7

oppression: articulation of, 42–44; and bitch feminism, 27, 29, 39; and enslavism, 17; and feminism, 94–95, 101; and global mother feminism, 87; and mean girl feminism, 7–8, 21–23, 94; and racialized meanness, 97; and white feminism, 7–8, 17–18, 45, 54, 56, 98; and white womanhood, viii, x, 9, 19, 46

Ora, Rita, 28

Orci, Taylor, 35

On the Origins of the Women's Liberation Movement (Joreen), 29–32

othering and otherness, 9, 28, 33, 48–49, 76, 86

Ouellette, Laurie, 79

Palin, Sarah, 5, 22, 76–82, 89–90, 93, 117n10, 117n14

Parker, Kathleen, 80

patriarchy: and bitch feminism, 25, 27, 38–39, 41, 92; and global mother feminism, 75; and mean girl feminism, xii, 7, 20, 51, 54–55, 60–61, 65, 91; and postfeminism, 44, 52; and power couple feminism, 93; and white feminism, 3–4, 9, 11, 44, 55–56, 92. *See also* cisheteropatriarchy

people of color: and bitch feminism, 28, 39, 92; and feminism, 5, 51; and knowledge, 42; and liberal war, 89; and mean girl feminism, x, xii, 23, 53–54; and meanness, 95–97, 101; and niceness, 108n60; and suffrage, 10; and white duplicity, 2; and white feminism, viii, ix, 7, 17–18, 22, 52, 81, 98, 100; and white supremacy, 55; and white womanhood, xi, 9, 15, 99

performativity: and agency, 18–19; and bitch feminism, 20, 25–37, 39–41, 92; and Laura Bush, 85, 87; and civility, 11, 13–14, 108n54; and embourgeoisement,

11; and feminism, xii, 5, 8, 101, 106n28; and global mother feminism, 22, 74, 76–77, 89, 93; and mean girl feminism, xii, 2–3, 7, 14, 22–23, 46, 49, 53, 55–57, 91–94, 99; and meanness, 7, 95; and postfeminism, 41, 56; and power couple feminism, 61, 68; and Sarah Palin, 78, 80; vs. racialized meanness, 97; and white feminism, 4, 20, 22, 30, 50–52, 91–92, 94, 97–99; and white womanhood, vii–viii, x, xi, 4, 7, 16, 18–19, 98–99

"personal is political," 72, 91, 98

phallic girls, 37–38

Pham, Minh-Ha, 87

pleasure, xii, 38, 40, 45–46, 50, 53, 63

politicians, 68–71, 76–80, 83–85

popular culture: and bitch feminism, 25–29, 37, 39, 51; and feminism, xi–xii, 4–6; and mean girl feminism, 1–2, 22, 46, 95; and postfeminism, 50–51; and power couple feminism, viii, 66, 69; and white feminism, xiii, 98

popular feminism, xi, 22, 29, 56, 60, 93, 104n12

postfeminism: and beauty, 41, 44, 51, 56; and bitch feminism, 37–38; and *Clueless*, 49–50; vs. feminism, 43, 45, 50–53, 56–57, 92–93; and mean girl feminism, 6, 20–21, 41, 43–44, 46, 50–51; and *Mean Girls*, 47–49; and Sarah Palin, 80; and white feminism, 41, 44–46, 56–57, 92–93; and white womanhood, 19, 49, 52

power: and agency, 18–19; and bitch feminism, 25, 31–32, 34–35, 38; and civility, 11–14, 108n54; and decolonial feminism, 100; and feminism, 101; and global mother feminism, 21, 75; in *Gossip Girl*, 64–65; and illegible rage, 45; and mean girl feminism, xii, 2–3, 23, 48, 50, 57, 60, 67, 91, 94; and postfeminism, 43–44, 53, 56; and power couple feminism, 62, 71, 93; and racialized meanness, 96; and vulnerability, 110n7; and white feminism, viii, xiii, 7, 15, 26, 46, 52, 89–90; and white womanhood, 8, 94

power couple feminism, 21, 57–61; and civility, 14, 57; and Hillary and Bill Clinton, 61–62, 69–73; and envy, 60–62, 72–73, 93; in *Gossip Girl*, 61–68, 73; and

mean girl feminism, 8, 61, 68, 72; and monogamy, 63; and politicians, 68–69; in popular culture, viii, 66, 69; vs. racialized meanness, 96; and white womanhood, 19, 58–61, 73

prestige, white, 4, 10–11, 27, 64, 105n15

private vs. public spheres, 59, 66–67, 69–70, 72, 81, 84, 91

privilege: and bitch feminism, 37; and feminism, 16, 101; and global motherhood, 22, 79, 82; and mean girl feminism, x, 2, 55; usage of term, 105n15; and white feminism, xiii, 10–11, 14, 16, 54, 82; and white womanhood, xi, 8–9

progress: and bitch feminism, 27, 29, 33; and embourgeoisement, 11, 17; and global mother feminism, 77, 86, 88–89; and mean girl feminism, 7, 94, 99; and militarism, 86; and power couple feminism, 59–60, 63, 100; and white feminism, 14, 22, 38, 45, 55, 81, 93, 98

protest, viii, 3–4, 6–7, 17, 34, 40, 52

queen bees, 47–49, 57, 60–62, 64, 93, 117n10

queer and trans people, 5–6, 10, 53, 74, 98

race: and bitch feminism, 34, 39, 92; and global mother feminism, 77; and mean girl feminism, 57, 97; and Sarah Palin, 81; and political campaigns, 79; in popular media, 112n36; and power couple feminism, 59, 68–69; and self-affirmation, 97; and white feminism, 5, 7, 9–11, 18, 54, 57, 92, 94, 98

racialization: and bitch feminism, 30, 34, 38, 40; and blackface, 28; and civility, 9; and mean girl feminism, viii, 3, 15, 20, 47–49; and white feminism, 7, 15–16, 45, 48, 56

racialized people. *See* people of color

racism, 3–4, 9–11, 28, 30, 86, 90, 94, 98

rage, illegible, 20; and Karen meme, vii–viii; and mean girl feminism, 49, 51, 53–55, 92; and *Mean Girls*, 47–48; and postfeminism, 44; and white feminism, 45, 53, 56–57

rage, white, viii, 2, 21, 41, 117n14. *See also* anger

Raha, Maria, 87

rape, 15, 66–67, 79, 116n23

Real Housewives franchise, 34, 51

vernacular, 39–40, 42, 44, 47, 81, 95, 101
victimized status, x, 1, 9, 11, 17, 49, 88, 101
Vincent, Lynn, 77
violence and aggression: in Afghanistan,
120n69; and bitch feminism, 33, 38;
and Black womanhood, 29; and civility,
12–14; culture of, 3–4; and decolonial
feminism, 101; and global mother feminism, 75–77, 82, 85, 88–90; and mean
girl feminism, viii, xii, 3, 7, 48–50, 57,
61, 65–68; and power couple feminism,
21, 57, 60–63, 71–73, 93; and racialized
meanness, 96; and white feminism, viii,
6, 22, 91, 94, 99; and white womanhood,
15, 98
virtue, 2, 26, 35, 38, 48, 50, 61, 93, 99, 101
visibility, 5, 60–62, 71, 79, 88, 94, 96
vulnerability: and bitch feminism, 26; and
mean girl feminism, viii, 14; and power,
110n7; and white feminism, 8, 11, 15, 18,
91; and white womanhood, 8, 15–16, 98,
108n60

Ware, Vron, 10
War on Terror, 76–77, 83–89
Watson, Robert P., 85
Weheliye, Alexander, 6, 8, 15, 34, 43,
108n54
Weiner, Anthony, 72
Weiss, Joanna, 78
Westmoreland, Kalene, 26
Westwick, Ed, 61, 66–67, 116n23
What Men Want, 95–96
white feminism, viii–ix, xii–xiii; and bitch
feminism, 25–41, 92; future of, 98–101;
and global mother feminism, 8, 74–90,
93; and mean girl feminism, 6, 46–57,
92, 94; and postfeminism, 41, 44–46,
56–57, 92–93; and power couple
feminism, 58–73, 93, 100; vs. racialized
meanness, 96–98
white men: and bitch feminism, 33, 35–38,
92; and global mother feminism, 75, 93;
and mean girl feminism, 14; and power
couple feminism, 21, 57–61, 63, 67–68,
72–73; and slavery, 9, 34; and white
feminism, ix, 7, 10, 81

whitestream media, 28–29, 39
white supremacy: and bitch feminism, 29;
and civility, 14–15; and enslavism, 17;
and family values, 69; and global mother
feminism, 75; and mean girl feminism,
2; and Sarah Palin, 81; and postfeminism, 50; and power couple feminism,
73; and white feminism, 9–10, 17–18,
54, 82; and white womanhood, 9, 55
white womanhood, xi, 105n5; and agency,
19, 94; and bitch feminism, 26–27, 29–
30, 33–34, 37–38, 40; and civility, 9; and
civilization, 89–90; and embourgeoisement, 4–5, 10–11, 15; and family values,
4, 9, 54, 69; and gender, 5, 98; and global
mother feminism, 75, 77, 89–90; and
illegible rage, 53, 56; and imperialism,
84; and intersectionality, xi; and mean
girl feminism, xii, 1–3, 13–14, 23, 49,
54, 57, 91–94; and nationalism, 108n66;
and neoliberalism, 104n3; and niceness,
108n60; and oppression, viii, x, 9, 19,
46; performativity of, vii–viii, x, xi, 4, 7,
16, 18–19, 98–99; and postfeminism, 19,
49, 52; and power couple feminism, 19,
58–61, 73; and vulnerability, 8, 15–16, 98,
108n60; and white supremacy, 9, 55
Wiegman, Robyn, 5
willfulness, 36, 99
Wiseman, Rosalind, 46
Women, genre of, 16, 27, 29
women of color, 4, 12, 17, 22, 25, 27, 51, 93,
95–97
women's liberation movement, 29–32
women's rights, 17, 50, 83, 86–88
work-life balance, ix, 4, 21, 38, 54, 60–61,
63, 93
Wynter, Sylvia, 16

Yang, K. Wayne, 32
Yarrow, Allison, 26
Yeğenoğlu, Meyda, 88
Yoho, Ted, 25
Young M.A, 25

Zakaria, Rafia, 16, 39, 51, 76, 81, 93
Zolciak, Kim, 34

KIM HONG NGUYEN is an associate professor of
communication arts at the University of Waterloo
and the editor of *Rhetoric in Neoliberalism*.

Feminist Media Studies

The University of Illinois Press
is a founding member of the
Association of University Presses.

———————————————————

Composed in 11.25/13 Garamond Premier Pro
with Avenir LT Std display
by Lisa Connery
at the University of Illinois Press
Manufactured by Versa Press, Inc.

University of Illinois Press
1325 South Oak Street
Champaign, IL 61820-6903
www.press.uillinois.edu